LONDON
UP CLOSE

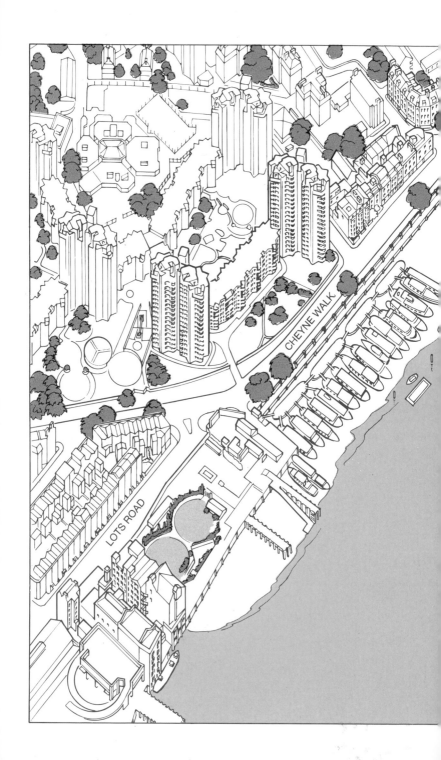

CHELSEA
REACH

LONDON UP CLOSE

DISTRICT TO DISTRICT, STREET BY STREET

Written by Fiona Duncan, Leonie Glass and Caroline Sharpe

Maps created by Irwin Technical

PASSPORT BOOKS
a division of *NTC Publishing Group*
Lincolnwood, Illinois USA

This edition first published in 1992 by Passport Books,
Trade Imprint of NTC Publishing Group, 4255 West Touhy Avenue,
Lincollnwood (Chicago), Illinois 60646-1975 U.S.A.

Conceived, edited and designed by
Duncan Petersen Publishing Ltd,
54, Milson Road,
London W14 0LB

Filmset by SX Composing, Rayleigh, Essex
Printed by Mateu Cromo, Madrid, Spain.
Cover photo: Zefa — U.K./H. Armstrong Roberts

Every reasonable care has been taken to ensure the information in this
guide is accurate, but the publishers and copyright holders can accept no
responsibility for the consequences of errors in the text or on the maps,
especially those arising from closures, or those topographical changes
occurring after completion of the aerial survey on which the maps are based.

Second printing 1994

ACKNOWLEDGEMENTS

The authors would like to thank the many people who have helped them with their research. Dozens of people gave information about buildings they live or work in; the London Tourist Board & Convention Bureau and the City of London Information Centre gave invaluable help; and of the many publications consulted in the course of writing, the authors particularly acknowledge:

The London Encyclopaedia, ed. Ben Weinreb and Christopher Hibbert (Macmillan); *In London* (Nicholson Publications); *The American Express Pocket Guide to London* (Mitchell Beazley); *Economist Business Traveller's Guides: London* (Collins); *Geoffrey Fletcher's London*, Geoffrey Fletcher (Penguin); *The Streets of London*, S. Fairfield (Papermac); *The Buildings of England, London: The Cities of London and Westminster*, Bridget Cherry and Nikolaus Pevsner; *Guide to The Architecture of London*, Edward Jones (Weidenfeld); *London Statues*, Arthur Byron (Constable); *The Blue Plaque Guide to London* (Journeyman Press); *Louise Nicholson's Definitive Guide to London*, Louise Nicholson (The Bodley Head); *The Blue Guide to London*, ed. Ylva French (A & C Black); *London Pub Guide* (Nicholson Publications); *Companion Guide to London*, David Piper (Collins); *A Wanderer in London*, E. V. Lucas (Methuen); *Naked City*, David Brazil (Queen Anne Press); *London, 2000 Years of a City and its People*, Felix Barker and Peter Jackson (Papermac); *Chelsea Seen from its Earliest Days*, John Bignell; (Hale); *The City of London*, James Bartholomew (Herbert Press); *The Markets of London*, Alec Forshaw and Theo Bergstrom (Penguin); *Wren's London*, Colin Amery (Lennard Publishing); *Nairn's London*, Ian Nairn (Penguin); *London Museums and Collections* (CP Guidebooks); *London's Riverside: From Hampton Court in the West to Greenwich Palace in the East*, Suzanne Ebel and Doreen Impey (Luscombe); *Michelin Tourist Guide to London* (Michelin). *400 Glorious Pubs*, John Thirkell (Imprint).

Finally, we would especially like to thank Anja Kutscher for painstakingly double-checking our facts by tramping the streets of London.

Editorial

Editor	Fiona Duncan
Assistant editor	Laura Harper
Index	Rosemary Dawe

Design

Art director Mel Petersen
Designers Chris Foley and Beverley Stewart

Aerial survey by Aerofilms Ltd, Boreham Wood, Hertfordshire
Maps created by Irwin Technical Ltd, 10-18, Clifton Street, London EC2A 4BT

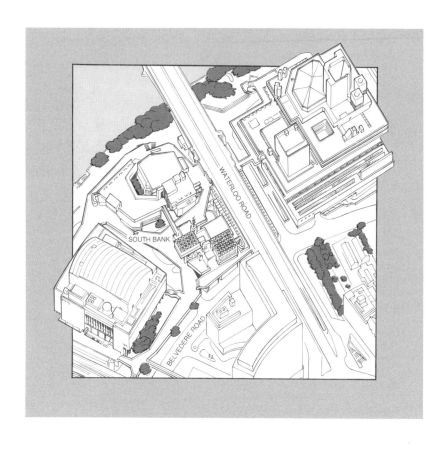

Contents

London bus routes

How the mapping was made

Isometric mapping is produced from aerial photographic surveys. One was specially commissioned for *3D London:* the helicopter flew at about 1,500 feet, with the camera angled at 45°. Weather conditions had to be slightly overcast in order to achieve maximum detail on the buildings.

Scores of enlargements were made from the negatives, which Irwin Technical, a group of technical illustrators in London (address on page 5), then used to create the maps. A team of seven, working in pen and ink, took well over 1,000 hours to complete the task.

'Isometric' projection means that verticals are the same height, whether in the foreground or the background – at the 'front' (bottom) of the page or at the 'back' (top). Thus the diminishing effect of perspective is avoided and all the buildings, whether near or distant, are shown in similar detail and appear at an appropriate height.

The order of the maps

The map squares are arranged in sequence running from north to south and from west to east. For further details, see the master location maps on pages 8-21.

Numerals on maps

Each numeral on a map cross refers to the text printed down the right hand border of the map. The numbers generally read from the top left of each map to the bottom right, in a west-east direction. However, there are deviations from this pattern when several interesting features occur close together, or within one street.

Opening and closing times

If a museum, display or exhibition is open during regular working hours, opening and closing times are not mentioned in the text accompanying the maps. Brief details are however given when opening times are irregular. In the case of historic or otherwise interesting buildings, assume that you cannot gain access to the interior unless opening times are mentioned.

Prices

£   means one person can eat for less than £15.
££   means one person can eat for less than £20.
£££   means one person generally pays more than £20.
Wine is not included.

Coverage

No guide book can cover everything of interest in London. This one contains a particularly wide range of information, and the writers concentrated on aspects of the city brought out by the special nature of the mapping, with emphasis on historical or general information that helped explain the fabric, evolution and working of the city. They have also tended to draw attention to the outstanding, even the peculiar, sometimes at the expense of the obvious and well-established, in the belief that this best reveals the essential character of a city. There is, in addition, much about eating, drinking, shopping and other practical matters.

Master location maps

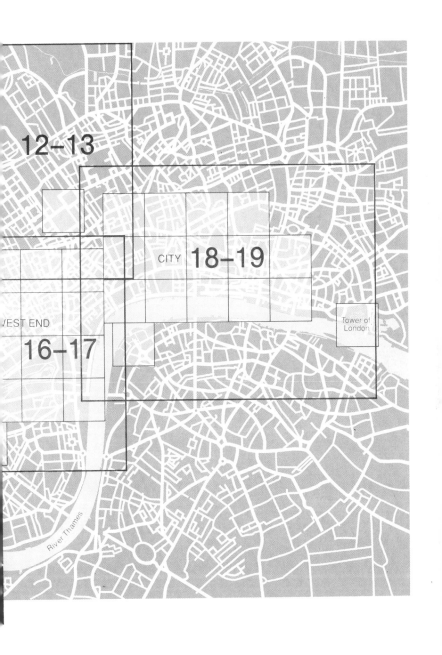

12–13

CITY 18–19

WEST END
16–17

Tower of London

River Thames

Master location maps

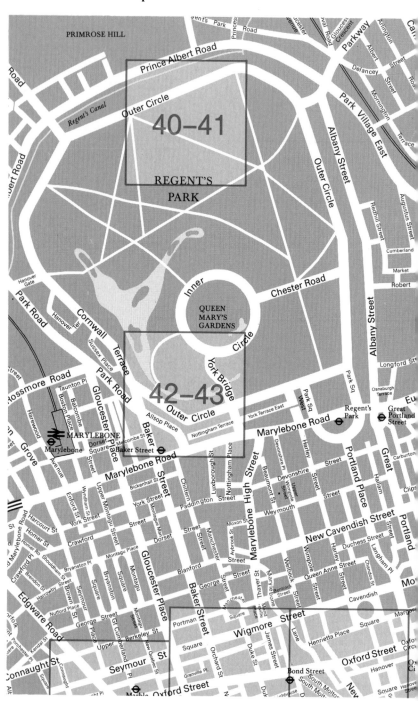

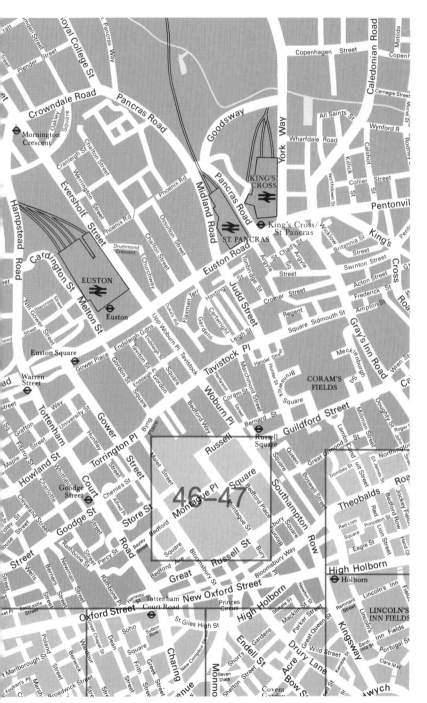

Master location maps

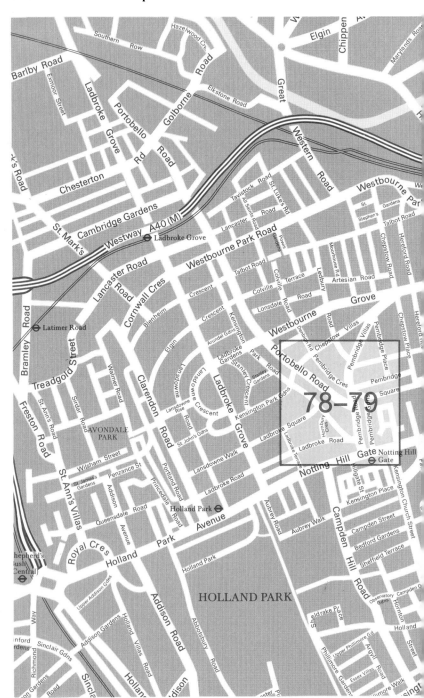

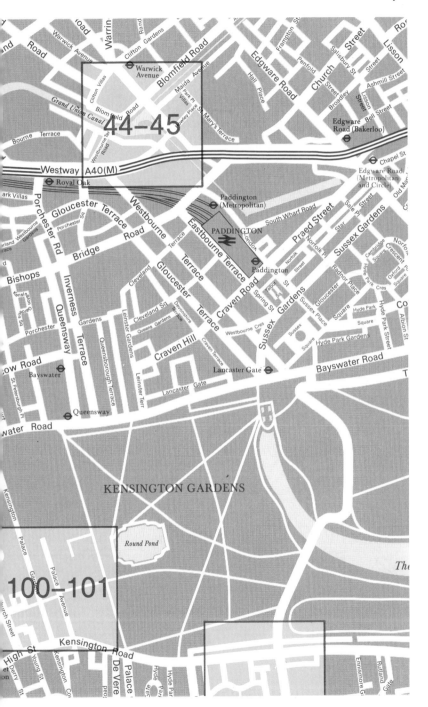

Master location maps

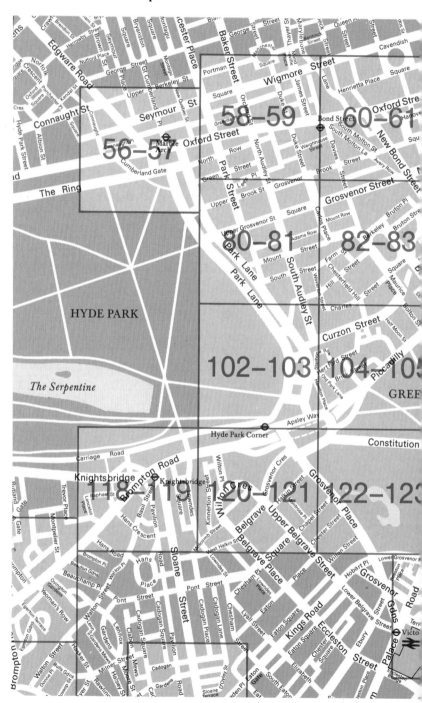

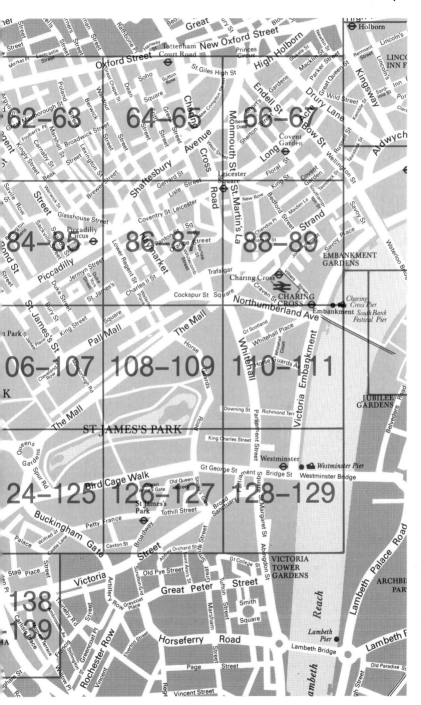

Master location maps

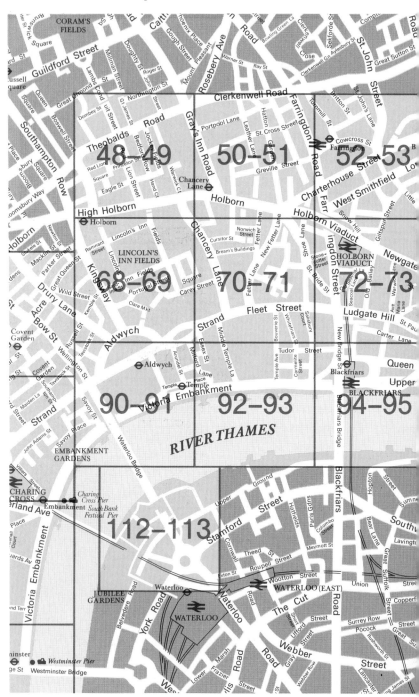

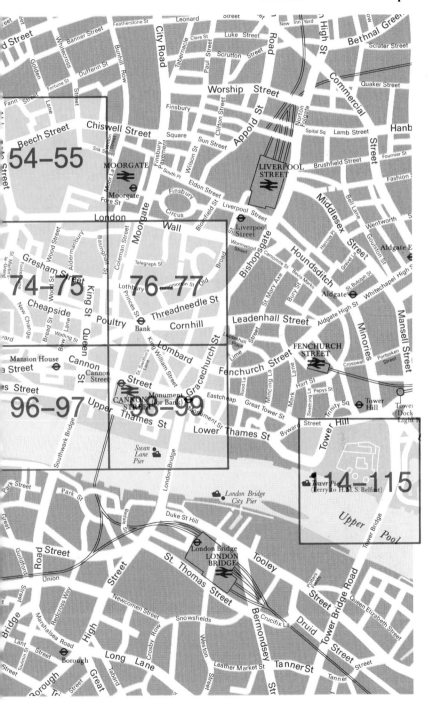

Master location maps

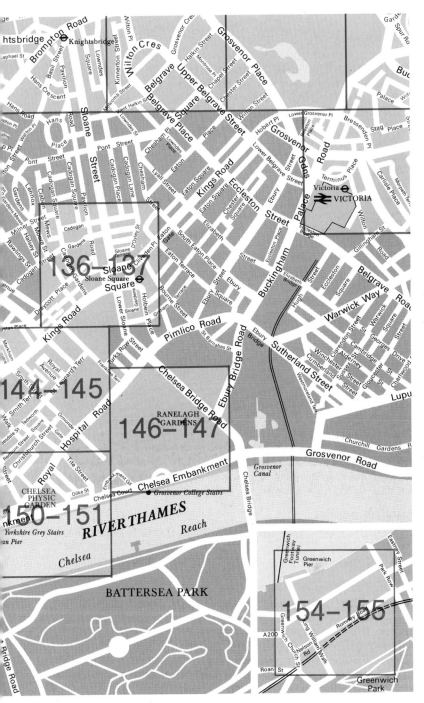

Transport

From airports to city

Heathrow is served by underground (tube), buses and taxis.

The London Underground's Piccadilly Line (connected to airport terminals by a moving walkway) takes passengers direct from its Heathrow stations (separate stops for terminal 4 and for terminals 1, 2 and 3) to central London, whence you can transfer to any other tube line (see map on pages 36-37). It operates between 5 am (6.45 on Sun) and 11.30 pm.

If you have more luggage than you can comfortably manage on the tube, a bus may be preferable. London Transport operates its Airbus services A1 and A2 between 6.20 am and 10.20 pm to Victoria or Euston Stations, calling at various central London points on the way.

Taxis are plentiful, though they are an expensive alternative, costing not less than £20 to central London. Ignore cab drivers touting for work inside the terminals; always go to an official rank.

For car drivers, central London is approached on the M4 motorway, and the drive usually takes about 30 minutes, though it can take much longer depending on the traffic (worst during rush-hour). When driving to Heathrow, you should leave the motorway at junction 3 for the new terminal 4 (signposted), and junction 4 for terminals 1, 2 and 3.

Gatwick is near Crawley in Surrey, some 25 miles from central London, about one hour by car along the M23 motorway. There is an excellent train service, the Gatwick Express, between the airport and Victoria Station, running every 15 minutes during the day and evening, and hourly throughout the night. The 777 Green Line bus service runs approximately every hour between 4.20 am and 10 pm to Victoria Coach Station and takes about 1½ hours.

If you intend to leave your car at Heathrow or Gatwick for more than a short time, remember to leave time to park it in one of the long-term car parks (a bus service to the airport is provided). Short-term car parks are close to the terminals but also very expensive.

London buses

'Just hop on a bus' may seem rather a daunting epithet to first-time visitors to London, faced with the complex route system. In reality, the system is fairly straightforward, and cheaper and more fun than the tube, though much slower. Red double-decker buses, each displaying a number, run along correspondingly numbered routes; check which route you want from the chart on pages 38-39. Their timing can be somewhat erratic (timetables displayed at bus stops should not be relied on), and they are notorious for always appearing in groups of three after a long interval. Bus stops display the numbers of the buses which call there. If the stop has the word 'request', the bus will only halt if a passenger on the bus rings the bell, or someone at the stop raises their hand. The conductor (or, on some buses, the driver) will collect your fare; the amount varies depending on how far you are travelling. Buses run from about 5 am to 11.30 pm, with night buses on selected routes. All major night bus routes pass through Trafalgar Square.

Some buses stop short of the end of their route; look at the front of the bus as it approaches to see where it is destined to stop, and check that it is far enough for you; other people in the queue will usually help.

In addition to the traditional double-decker buses, London Transport has recently introduced small single-decker buses called hoppers. These operate on central London routes, for example between South Kensington and Waterloo (No. C1), and are designed for people who want to travel only a couple of stops or so.

The London Underground

London's tube stations are by and large depressing, even squalid. They could well do with an expensive overhaul to bring them up to the standards of, say, the Paris Metro. Trains are often overcrowded, especially at rush-hours. The Underground network, however, is extensive and the system efficient, and it is a fast way of getting about the city. Each station is on at least one of nine Underground lines. These are featured by the map on page 36, printed in black and white (whereas tube maps displayed on the Underground itself are in colour, with a different colour to identify each line). In central London particularly, a station may be served by several lines, and this makes it easy to change from one line to another. To trace your route, and where you should, if necessary, change trains, simply follow the lines from the station from which you depart to your destination. Trains run daily from around 5.30 am (7.30 am on Sunday) to around midnight.

Stations are identified at street level by the London Transport symbol of a red circle cut by a blue horizontal line. Tickets can be bought at machines or, if you are in doubt, from the ticket office, where you should state your destination. Keep your ticket until it is collected at the end of your journey.

For details of both bus and tube routes, timetables and fares (including various special tickets and flat-rate passes) you can telephone 222 1234. London Transport have Travel Information Centres at Victoria, St James's Park, Oxford Circus, Piccadilly Circus, Euston, King's Cross and Heathrow tube stations. Free tube and bus maps are available from any Underground ticket office.

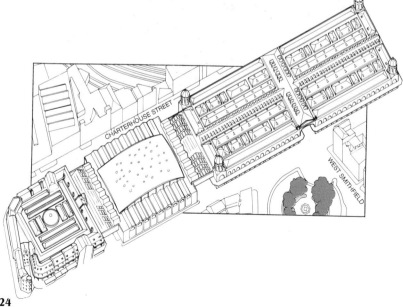

Taxis

Londoners who find themselves in foreign cities such as New York are usually terrified by the indigenous taxi drivers, who appear to have scant regard either for traffic regulations or for human life. By contrast, London cabbies are superb drivers, and neither they nor their famous stately black taxis are given to flashy manoeuvres. They also know their way about town and have had to pass an exam on the subject, known as 'the knowledge'. If you are not at a taxi rank (outside stations, large stores and so on) you can hail a taxi in the street, if its yellow 'For Hire' sign is illuminated above the windscreen. The fare is shown on the meter. You should add a 10-15 per cent tip, though to save time, cabbies prefer it if you simply round up the fare and say "Keep the change". Under £5 add approximately 50p, over £5 add about £1. Sometimes the drivers can be difficult about taking their 'fares' to destinations to which they don't want to go; remember that they are obliged to take you if the destination is within six miles of the pick-up point. If you wish to order a taxi by phone, there are several numbers to call including Computer Cab (286 0286), Radio Taxis (272 0272) and Dial-a-Cab (253 5000). If you leave something behind in a taxi, try calling in at the taxi lost property office at 15 Penton Street, N1.

The phrase 'black cab' to denote a licensed taxi with a meter is becoming confusing, since licensed cabbies are starting to drive a new make of taxi called Metrocab which, apart from looking different, appears in several different colours. The much-loved black cab may soon be a thing of the past.

Unlicensed taxis are not to be recommended unless you know a reputable company. They are usually ordinary saloon cars (often scruffy) and are referred to as minicabs. They are frequently unreliable, and finding your destination may prove a problem. As minicabs don't have meters, the fare must be agreed on at the start of the trip.

Private Cars

Driving is becoming increasingly problematic in London: traffic is slow moving on most main roads, and blockages can often occur in side streets. For newcomers, the street layout is confusing and complicated. Courtesy amongst drivers is not unknown; certainly, they are not as aggressive as in Rome, Paris or Madrid.

Apart from remembering to drive on the left and obeying traffic regulations (laid out in the Highway Code, available from HMSO Bookshop, 49 High Holborn, WC1. There are three rules of which you should be particularly aware: **1** Don't drink and drive. More than about three glasses of wine, or their equivalent, will send you over the limit on the breathalyser which police carry for on-the-spot checks on suspicious motorists. **2** Wear seat belts. Police can impose fines if they see drivers and front-seat passengers without their seat belts fastened. **3** Don't park illegally. Parking on single or, more dangerously, double yellow lines can, and frequently does, result in a traffic warden giving you a parking ticket for which you have to pay a fine, or in your car being clamped or towed away. The latter two evils involve much inconvenience, several hours of your time and well in excess of £60 of your money. Better to endeavour to find an empty parking meter (difficult in central London; don't let the meter run into 'excess time' or again you may be fined) or park in an NCP car park. To find one, follow the blue 'parking' signs.

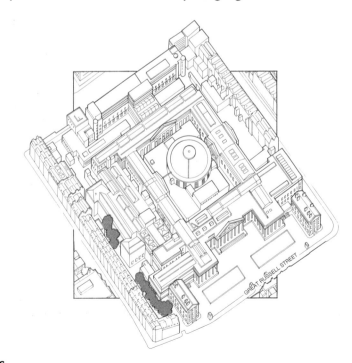

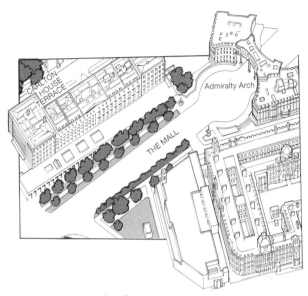

Visiting Britain

By train London's main British Rail stations ring the city, and link the capital with all major towns in Britain through the fast Inter-City service, as well as Motorail and sleeper trains. The main stations are Paddington (information tel. 262 6767), serving south-west England and south Wales; Charing Cross, Waterloo and Victoria (tel. 928 5100), serving the south and south-east; Liverpool Street (tel. 283 7171), serving Cambridge and East Anglia; Euston and St Pancras (tel. 387 7070), serving the Midlands, North Wales, the north-west and west Scotland; King's Cross (tel. 278 2477), serving the north-east and east Scotland.

In addition to the Underground, London's suburbs are served by British Rail's Network SouthEast service. Journeys further afield are made on the main line network, departing from London's British Rail main line stations.

By air British Airways (tel. 897 4000 for flight times and reservations) and British Midland (tel. 589 5599) offer 'shuttle' services between Heathrow and Manchester, Edinburgh, Glasgow and Belfast airports. As well as these two main operators, several other companies offer scheduled flights to Britain's 30 or so regional airports. For details, contact a travel agent, such as Thomas Cook (1 Marble Arch, W1; tel. 402 9424, and many other branches).

London City Airport, situated in Docklands on the east of the city, and opened in 1987, is a 'stolport' (short take off/landing), mainly suited to businessmen. For information on which British and European cities are currently served, tel. 474 5555.

By coach National Express is the largest coach company in Britain. Victoria Coach Station is the London terminus for their services to al parts of the country. It is a slow, but inexpensive way of travelling. For details of services and fares tel. 730 0202.

By car Britain's toll-free motorway network is extensive, reaching most parts of the country, and where 'A' (major) and 'B' (secondary) roads may provide the shortest route, the motorway is usually quicker. The speed limit on motorways and dual carriageways is 70 mph (110 kmph), 60 mph (100 kmph) on single carriageways and 30 mph (50 kmph) in built-up areas. Be warned that many motorways, most notoriously the M1, are plagued by 'cone disease', with long sections subjected to contra-flow systems, marked by a series of orange cones, caused by road-works. Long delays can occur at these places. Motorways from all directions converge on London, now all linked by the M25 motorway which rings the city. An inner ring is formed by the A205 South Circular and A406 North Circular. Approaching London, once off the motorway, the driver is plunged bewilderingly into the suburbs. If in doubt, for central London, follow signs for the 'West End'.

For further information on travelling in Britain, you can visit the British Travel Centre, 4-12 Lower Regent Street, SW1; tel. 730 3400.

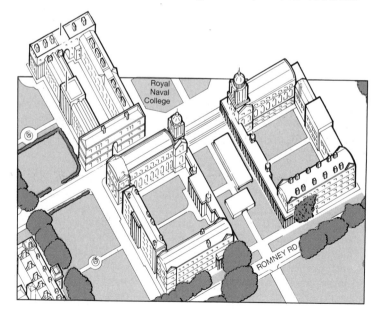

Useful data

Tourist information

London Tourist Board information centres are located at:

- Victoria Station forecourt, SW1; open daily summer 9 am-10.30 pm, winter 9 am-7 pm (5 pm on Sun).
- Harrods, Knightsbridge, SW1 (4th floor); open during store hours.
- Selfridges, Oxford Street, W1 (basement services arcade); open during store hours.
- Tower of London, West Gate, EC3; open summer only, daily 10 am to 6 pm.
- Heathrow, terminals 1, 2 and 3, Underground Station concourse, Heathrow Airport; open daily, 9 am-6 pm.
- Heathrow, terminal 2, Arrivals concourse, Heathrow Airport; open daily 9 am-7 pm.

Telephone information, including daily events, can be obtained by dialling 730 3488 between 9 am and 6 pm.

For children's events, call Kidsline on 222 8070 between 4 and 6 pm in term time, and 9 am and 4 pm in holidays.

Disabled visitors can receive guidance from the Disabled Information Service run by RADAR (Royal Association for Disability and Rehabilitation) on 637 5400.

Sightseeing tours

London Transport's double-decker Round London Sightseeing Tour bus departs every half hour daily, except bank holidays, from Piccadilly Circus, Marble Arch, Baker Street and Victoria Street. Tickets can be bought on the bus, but they are cheaper if purchased from any London Transport or London Tourist Board information centre (cut-price, direct-entry tickets to Madame Tussauds also included). Circular tour lasts 1½ hours; buses are open-topped in summer: tel. 227 3456. Cityrama tours also depart every 30 minutes daily, except Christmas Day, from Trafalgar Square, Piccadilly Circus, Lower Regent Street, Westminster Abbey and Grosvenor Gardens, and provide eight-language taped commentaries: tel. 720 6663. Most luxurious is the Harrods half- or full-day tour, also with an eight-language commentary: tel. 581 3603.

Apart from Harrods, various other companies offer luxury coach tours, with stop-offs for guided visits round London's principal sights, or for river-boat cruises:

- ■ Evan Evans, 27 Cockspur Street, SW1; tel. 730 3477.
- ■ Frames Rickards, 11 Herbrand Street, WC1; tel. 837 3111.
- ■ Golden Tours, 132 Cromwell Road, SW7; tel. 743 3300.

All can be booked through the London Tourist Board Centres at Victoria, Harrods or Selfridges.

River trips Boats run frequently every day from Westminster and Charing Cross piers to the Tower and Greenwich, and in summer further downstream to the Thames Barrier and upstream to Kew or Hampton Court. For further information, fares and departure times, contact the recorded River Boat Information Service, tel. 730 4812; also Thames Line Riverbus Service, tel 987 0311.

Walking tours The following companies organize morning or afternoon theme walks in various parts of London:

- ■ Discovering London; tel. (0277) 213704.
- ■ London Walks; tel. 441 8906.
- ■ Citisights of London; tel. 739 2372.
- ■ Cockney Walks; tel. 504 9159.

Private guided tours For a guide plus car call either Take a Guide; tel. 221 5475, or British Tours; tel. 629 5267.

Shopping, banking and business hours

Generally speaking, shops in central London are open between 9 or 9.30 am and 5 to 6 pm, Mon-Sat. Fashion and gift shops may not open until 10 am. Some specialist shops are closed on Sat, or open only in the mornings. Outside the city centre, some shops close between 1 and 2 pm for lunch and for one afternoon a week, usually on Wed or Thur. In central London most shops stay open one evening a week for 'late-night' shopping. Oxford Street shops stay open until 8 pm on Thur, and Knightsbridge and King's Road shops stay open until 7 pm on Wed. Certain chains of food stores have very late opening hours, as well as some small corner shops. Giant supermarkets such as Sainsbury's and Safeway stay open at least until 8 pm; and on some nights as late as 10 pm.

On Sunday, some newsagents are open in the mornings, also the occasional grocery store or delicatessen, and some large supermarkets.

Banks are open from 9.30 am; some close at 5.30 pm, others earlier, Mon-Fri. A few bank branches open on Saturday. In central London they are: Barclays at 140-142 King's Road, SW3, 74 Kensington High Street, W8 and also at 28 Hampstead High Street, NW3 – all open 9.30 am-12 noon; National Westminster at 466 Oxford Street, W1 and 250 Regent Street, W1, open 9.30 am-12.30 pm; and Lloyds at 399 Oxford Street, W1 and at Selfridges, Oxford Street, W1 between 10 am-3 pm and 9 am and 5 pm respectively.

Bureaux de change (poorer exchange rates than banks) have longer opening hours, and can be found at airports and stations, as well as in some Underground stations and main shopping streets.

There are several 24-hour bureaux de change, for example Chequepoint at Marble Arch, Earl's Court Road and Queensway.

'Nine to five' are the normal working hours for office workers, although many stay longer and City workers are particularly early risers. The 'rush-hour' occurs between about 8 and 9.30 am and 5 and 7 pm, Mon-Fri.

Public holidays

It feels like a Sunday, with banks and shops closed, on the following days of the year: New Year's Day (1 January), Good Friday, Easter Monday, May Day (first Mon in May), Spring Bank Holiday (last Mon in May), August Bank Holiday (last Mon in August), Christmas Day (25 December), Boxing Day (26 December).

The post

Main post offices are open from 9 am to 5.30 pm, Mon-Fri, and 9 am to 1 pm on Sat. The post office in William IV Street, off Trafalgar Square, is an exception, open from 8 am to 8 pm Mon-Sat and from 10 am to 5 pm on Sun. The opening hours of sub post offices vary; they often form part of newsagents or corner stores. Parcels should be taken to post offices for weighing; various special postal services – such as Recorded Delivery and Red Star – are available. Stamps are bought at post offices, and letters are posted in the red pillar-boxes that dot the streets, or in less conspicuous wall-mounted post-boxes. Sending mail by first-class post is recommended, since it is faster, more reliable and only a few pence dearer than second class.

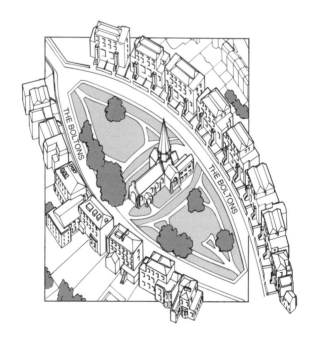

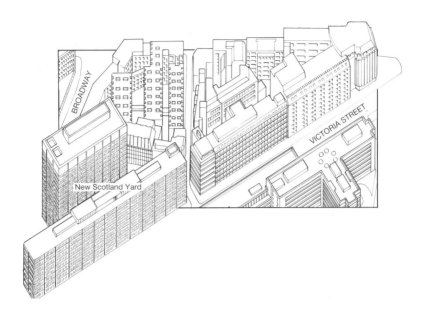

Telephones

The old-style red telephone boxes have almost entirely been replaced by new black and yellow ones (also silver and blue or silver and green). All have clear instructions on how to use them and can be found on streets, in stations, large shops, public buildings and pubs. Some take coins, others take credit cards, or 'Phonecards' which can be bought in post offices and shops displaying the Phonecard sign.

There are two dialling codes for London: 071 for central London numbers; 081 for greater London numbers. These prefixes are added to the existing numbers whether dialling from outside London, or from greater to central London or vice versa. Most numbers in this guide have 071 prefixes.

Some call boxes contain the local – in this case London – telephone directories, with information about codes and operator services printed in the front of the A-K book. Here are some useful numbers:

- For help from an operator dial 100.
- For the international operator dial 155.
- For directory enquiries dial 142 or 192.
- For international directory enquiries dial 153.
- To send a Telemessage within the UK or to the USA dial 190.
- For international telegrams dial 193.
- For the speaking clock dial 123.
- For the Weatherline (south-east England weather forecast) dial 246 8091.
- In an emergency, dial 999 for the police, ambulance and fire services. The call is free; you will be asked which service you require.

Publications

The weekly magazines *Time Out* and *City Limits* have comprehensive listings of entertainments and events, including pop and classical concerts. The *Evening Standard*, a daily evening paper, contains details of theatres and cinemas, and *The Times* and *The Independent* have good information.

The travel sections of book shops will reveal a wide range of guidebooks to London. For the disabled, Nicholson publishes *Access in London*, and a useful and inexpensive guide for children, *Children's London*. Good general bookshops include Hatchards at 187 Piccadilly, W1 and Waterstones at 121 Charing Cross Road, WC2 and other branches (open until 7.30 pm Mon-Fri, 7 pm on Sat also Sundays). The Pan Bookshop, 158 Fulham Road, SW10 is open till 10 pm Mon-Sat, 9 pm on Sun.

For your nearest public library, see under 'Libraries' in the telephone directory. The largest are: Westminster Central Reference Library, St Martin's Street, WC2, tel. 828 8070; and the Guildhall Library, Aldermanbury, EC2, tel. 606 3030.

Foreign embassies

Embassies, high commissions and consulates are listed in the telephone directory under 'Embassy', 'High Commissioner' and 'Consuls' or under the country's name. Here is a selection:

- **Australia** Australia House, Strand, WC2; tel. 379 4334.
- **Canada** 38 Grosvenor Street, W1; tel. 409 2071.
- **France** 58 Knightsbridge, SW1; tel. 235 8080.
- **Germany** 23 Belgrave Square, SW1; tel. 235 5033.
- **Ireland** 17 Grosvenor Place, SW1; tel. 235 2171.
- **Italy** 38 Eaton Place, SW1; tel. 236 9371.
- **Japan** 101-4 Piccadilly, W1; tel. 465 6500.
- **Netherlands** 38 Hyde Park Gate, SW7; tel. 584 5040.
- **New Zealand** 80 Haymarket, SW1; tel. 930 8422.
- **Spain** 20 Draycott Place, SW3; tel. 581 5921.
- **USA** 24 Grosvenor Square, W1; tel. 499 9000.

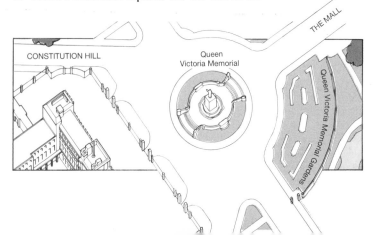

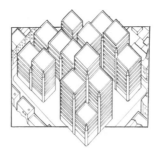

Medical information

Hospitals

The following hospitals are among those in London with 24-hour casualty departments: St Mary's, Praed Street, W2, tel. 725 6666; St Bartholomew's (Barts), West Smithfield, EC1, tel. 601 8888; Royal Free, Pond Street, NW3, tel. 794 0500; St Thomas', Lambeth Palace Road, SE1, tel. 928 9292; Westminster & Chelsea, Fulham Road, SW10, tel. 746 8000; Guy's, St Thomas Street, SE1, tel. 407 7600.

Late-night chemists

Chemists operate a duty rota for evenings and Sunday so that one chemist in each area will be open at these times; details in local papers. There are no 24-hour chemists in London, but Bliss Chemist, Willesden Lane, NW6, is open every day from 9 am to 2 am. Boots, Piccadilly, and some other central London branches are open until 8 pm Mon-Sat. Bliss Chemist, Marble Arch, is open 9 to midnight, Mon-Sun.

Doctors

Should you need to see a doctor, either (if your condition warrants it) for a home visit, or preferably at his or her surgery, consult the *Yellow Pages* telephone directory under the heading 'Doctors (Medical Practitioners)'. If you are an EEC resident, reciprocal health arrangements will make it easy for you to reclaim charges on your return, provided you have the necessary documentation before you travel. With non-EEC residents, the situation is more complex, and visitors are advised to consult health professionals at home before travelling. Full details are also given in the manual published by the Department of Health and Social Security entitled *NHS Treatment of Overseas Visitors*.

Dental treatment

A list of dentists will be found under 'Dental Surgeons' in the *Yellow Pages* telephone directory. For emergency treatment, you can go to Eastman Dental Hospital, 256 Gray's Inn Road, WC1, tel. 837 3646 (Mon-Fri, 9 am-4.30 pm); or to Guy's, St Thomas Street, SE1, tel. 407 7600 (daily 9 am-3.30 pm, Mon-Fri go to 23rd floor of the tower block, at weekends go to Casualty Department).

London Underground map

Page numbers of isometric maps on which the stations are featured

Key to lines

Bakerloo	East London	Piccadilly
Central	Jubilee	Victoria
Circle	Metropolitan	British Rail
District	Northern	Docklands Light Railway

○ Interchange stations

♯ Connections with British Rail

♯ Connections within walking distance

★ Closed Sundays

✠ Closed Saturdays and Sundays

◄ Served by Piccadilly line early mornings and late evenings Mondays to Saturdays and all day Sundays

† See poster maps at Underground stations for opening and closing times of these stations

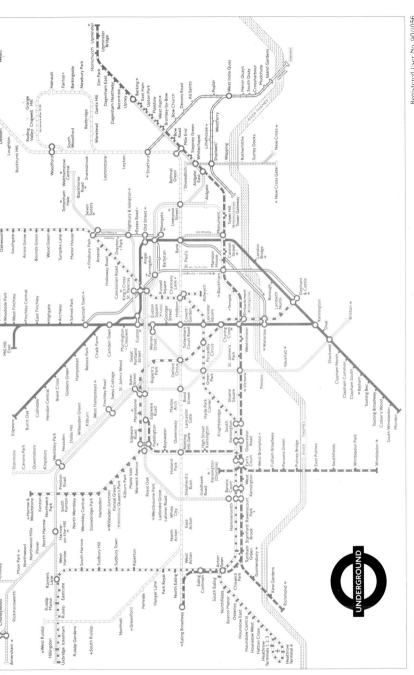

UNDERGROUND

37

London bus routes

From \ To	Aldwych	Angel	Baker Street	Bank	Chelsea/King's Road	Earl's Court	Elephant & Castle	Euston	Hammersmith	Hampstead	Highgate	High St Kensington	Holborn	Hyde Park Corner	Kew	King's Cross
Angel	4/171															
Baker Street	13	30														
Bank	6/11	43	6/13													
Chelsea/King's Road	11	22/38	22/30	11/22												
Earl's Court	30/9	74/38	30	74/25*	31											
Elephant & Castle	1/68	171	12/13	133	12/11	A										
Euston	68/77A	30/73	18/30	68/6	68/11	30	68									
Hammersmith	11	10/73	27	11	11	10/31	9/12	10								
Hampstead	24/15	24/30	24/6	24/30	24/1	24/30	24/1	24/30	24/10							
Highgate	134/176	43	134/30	43	134/22	134/30	134/1	134/73	134/10	210						
High St Kensington	9	10/73	27	9	31	31	9/12	10	9/10	73/10	10/134					
Holborn	68/77A	19/38	6/159	8/22B	22	22/30	68/188	68/77A	8/10	7/24	8/134	19/9				
Hyde Park Corner	9	19/73	30/74	9/25	19/22	30/74	9/12	10/73	9/10	73/24	73/134	9/10	19/22			
Kew	27/9	27/73	27	K	27/31	27/31	B	27/10	27	27/24	27/134	27	C	27/10		
King's Cross	77A	30/73	18/30	77A/6	30/22	30	45/63	30/73	10	C11	73/134	10	77A	10/73	10/27	
Knightsbridge	9	19/30	30/74	9/6	19/22	30/74	9/12	10/30	9/10	10/24	10/134	9/52	19/22	14/9	10/27	10/30
Liverpool Street	6/11	43+	6/159	6/8	11	25/30	35/133	6/68	11	8/24	22B/134	6/68	8/22B	9/11	D	6/77A
Ludgate Circus	6/15	4	15/13	6/11	11	9/30	45/63	11	15/24	17*	15/9	6/68	9/11	9/27	45/73	
Marble Arch	6/15	30/73	30/74	6/8	16/2	74	12	10/73	10	73/24	73/134	10	7/8	16/73	10/27	30/73
Monument	15/501*	43	15/159	43/133	15/11	E	35/133	15/68	15/11	15/24	43	15/501*	15/9	E	15/77A	
Notting Hill Gate	15/12	12/73	27	12/6	31	31	12	12/73	27	27/24	27/134	28/31	12/8	52	27	12/73
Olympia	9	10/73	27	9/6	9/31	73/31	9/12	10	10/27	10/24	10/134	9/10	9/8	9/10	27	10
Oxford Circus	6/15	73	13/159	6/8	73/22	73/30	12/53	10/73	10	73/24	73/134	10	7/8	10/73	10/27	10/73
Oxford St/Selfridges	6/15	73	13/159	6/8	73/22	74	12	10/73	10	73/24	73/134	10	7/8	10/73	10/27	10/73
Paddington	15	27/73	27	15/6	27/31	27/31	15/73	27/73	27	27/24	27/134	27	7	36/506*	27	27/73
Piccadilly Circus	6/9	19/38	13/159	6/15B*	19/22	9/30	12/53	14/14A	9	19/24	19/134	9	19/8	19/14	9/27	38/10
Richmond	27/9	27/73	27	K	27/31	27/31	B	27/10	27	27/24	27/134	27	C	27/10	27	27/10
St Paul's	6/15	4	15/13	6/11	11	25/30	141	6/68	11	15/24	17*	15/9	6/68	9/11	17*	
Sloane Square	11	19	19/74	11	11/22	19/30	11/12	11/73	11	19/24	22/1	C1	19/22	19/137	E	19/30
South Kensington	14/9	30	30/74	14/25*	14/219	30/74	45	14/30	49/10	30/24	14/1	49/C1	14/19	14/30	49/27	30
Tate Gallery/Millbank	77A	88/73	2A/2B	77A/11	36/30	36/30	510	77A	36/10	88/24	I	36/77A	2B/27	J	77A	
Tottenham Court Rd	176	73	8/13	8/22B	19/30	73/30	176	10/73	10	24	134	10	7/8	14/73	10/27	10/73
Trafalgar Square	6/9	15/171A	13	6/11	11	9/30	12/53	77/77A	9/11	24	29/134	9	77A	9	9/27	77A
Victoria	11	38/73	2A/2B	11/25*	11	36/30	510	73	11	24	73/134	52/C1	25/38	36/73	52/27	73
Warren Street	176	30/73	27/30	29/8	73/22	30	29/12	10/73	10/27	24	134	10/27	29/8	10/73	10/27	10/73
Waterloo	68/171A	4/171A	68/13	76/501*	11	C1/31	1/68	176/168	68/9	1/24	176/134	C1	68/171	68/27	C1/27	68/77A
Westminster	77/77A	29/73	159	11	11	C1/31	12/53	77/77A	11	24	29/134	C1	77/77A	12/9	C1/27	77A

NOTES: ★ Buses run Mon-Fri only. Some buses do not run on Sundays – check at bus stops
+ From Liverpool St walk along Eldon St to Moorgate for direct bus service (43)

The following journeys are difficult by bus, involving two changes and the alternative tube connections are suggested:

A Bakerloo line to Embankment then change to District line
B District line to Embankment then change to Bakerloo line
C District line to Earls Court then change to Piccadilly line
D Circle line to South Kensington then change to District line
E District line direct
F Escalator link to Bank then change to Northern line
G District line to South Kensington then change to Circle line
H Circle or District lines direct
I Victoria line from Pimlico to Warren Street then change to Northern line
J Victoria line from Pimlico to Victoria then change to District line
K District line to Monument then use escalator link

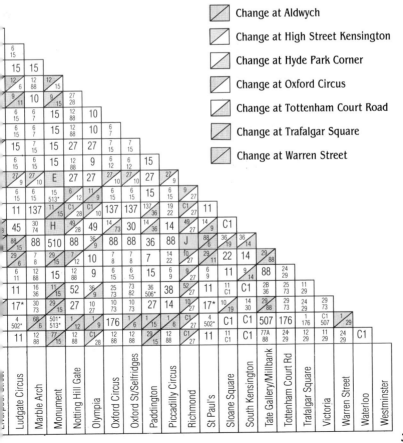

Change at Aldwych
Change at High Street Kensington
Change at Hyde Park Corner
Change at Oxford Circus
Change at Tottenham Court Road
Change at Trafalgar Square
Change at Warren Street

PRINCE ALBERT ROAD

GRAND UNION CANAL

② Regent's Canal

GRAND UNION CANAL

GRAND UNION CANAL

Giraffe House

OUTER CIRCLE

Mapplin Terraces

Reptile House

Zoological Gardens

Elephant and Rhino Pavillion

REGENT'S PARK

London Zoo

① Colloquially known as London Zoo, the **Zoological Gardens** were laid out by Decimus Burton in 1827, over five acres, to display the Zoological Society of London's collection of animals, and opened to a curious public in 1847. There are now over 8,000 animals occupying 36 acres of Regent's Park. London Zoo has often been the first to house animals outside their natural habitat: in 1843 the world's first reptile house opened there; the keeper tried unsuccessfully to charm a cobra, only to be bitten and die. Through the Society, which was founded in 1826 by Sir Thomas Stamford Raffles, the Zoo has become a world centre for scientific research. Its architecture reflects the changing views of the Society on the way animals should be kept: the Giraffe House (1836) is one of the few early buildings to survive. The Mappin Terraces (closed until money can be raised for redevelopment) were revolutionary when designed in 1913 by Belcher and Joass, with the idea that animals should range more freely, their cages hidden from view; latterly they appeared a harsh and unfriendly environment. The Penguin Pool, designed by Lubetkin and Tecton, is described by Pevsner as a *tour de force* derived from Le Corbusier. Since 1959, various architects have contributed to the redevelopment, including Sir Hugh Casson (Elephant and Rhino Pavilion), and J.W. Toovey (the new Lion Terraces). The most famous of the Zoo's buildings is the tangled-looking aviary designed by Lord Snowdon and opened in 1965. Plagued by financial problems, the Zoo has embarked on a ten-year plan to raise funds; a new children's zoo and macaw aviary have recently opened. The threat of extinction, however, despite calling itself the more politically correct 'conservation centre', is far from assuaged. ② **Regent's Canal**, part of the Grand Union Canal linking London and Birmingham, bisects the Zoo and allows a romantic form of transport to and fro. You can dine aboard the motor launch *My Fair Lady*, which cruises from Camden to Little Venice and back each evening (tel. 485 6210). The canal was opened in style in 1820, with architect John Nash sailing down in the City State Barge and brass bands playing. ③ **Broad Walk**, a stately tree-lined promenade connecting the Outer Circle. In it is the Parsee drinking fountain, a heady mixture of Victorian Gothic and the East, topped by a bust of Queen Victoria, which was donated by Sir Cowasjee Jahangir.

Marylebone Road/Regent's Park

① **Regent's Park** was once Henry VIII's hunting forest, and later its small-holdings provided London with hay and dairy produce. In 1811 the leases ran out, and the Crown seized the opportunity to develop the 500 acres of land. An architects' competition was launched and, thanks to the unswerving patronage of the Prince Regent, John Nash's brilliant design for a *rus in urbe* of majestic proportions won. His plan for two circles of terraces disguised as individual palaces, with 26 villas hidden in the landscaped parkland, was considerably modified, but Regent's Park remains a tribute to Nash's genius and foresight. Amongst its features are ② The **Boating Lake**, a focus for Sunday family life, with a band playing nearby; ③ **Queen Mary's Rose Gardens**, where intoxicating scents abound in summer, and the Open Air Theatre braves the weather to perform Shakespeare in a wonderfully atmospheric setting (two restaurants **£**); ④ **Clarence Terrace**, by Nash and Decimus Burton (Wilkie Collins lived at No. 2, later the home of Louis Macneice). ⑤ **Cornwall Terrace**, by Nash and Burton with, at No. 10, a glorious two-storey bow window decorated with caryatids, the British Academy at Nos 20-21; ⑥ **York Terrace**, designed by Nash as two separate terraces divided in the middle to allow a view of St Marylebone Church, with entrances at the back to preserve the illusion of two palaces. South of the park ⑦ the **Abbey National** tower block (1920s by J.J. Joass), incorporates 221B Baker Street, the fictional lodgings of Sherlock Holmes. ⑧ **The London Planetarium** gives you a guided tour of the planets in its permanent exhibition, Space Trail, and then uses its famous dome to take you on a magical, if neck-aching journey across the night sky; due to close for a major overhaul check. ⑨ Over-rated and plagued by queues, **Madame Tussauds** has drawn in the crowds to see its famous wax figures from past and present for well over 200 years. Figures are now grouped into themed areas, like 'The Garden Party' and there is a dark ride called 'The Spirit of London'. ⑩ A church has stood on this site since 1400. The present name of **St Marylebone** derives from the days when the church was called St Mary-by-the-Bourne, referring to the River Tyburn which ran beside. Built by Thomas Hardwick in 1813, the church has an eye-catching cupola and a cold blue, white and gold interior. Amongst many other luminaries, Byron and the daughter of Nelson and Lady Hamilton were christened in the church, and Robert Browning married Elizabeth Barrett here.

Warwick Avenue

CLIFTON VILLAS

WARWICK AVENUE

WARWICK PLACE

BLOMFIELD ROAD

WARWICK AVENUE

RANDOL

DELAMERE TERRACE

BLOMFIELD VILLAS

WESTBOURNE TERRACE ROAD

LITTLE VENICE

WARWICK CRESCENT

HARROW ROAD

WESTWAY

Little Venice

① **Clifton Villas**, probably named in celebration of Brunel's Clifton Suspension Bridge (1894). ② **Clifton Nurseries** (No. 5), largest in central London, boasting a vast selection from azaleas to kumquats, as well as attractive antique garden ornaments. ③ **Warwick Castle** (6 Warwick Place), Regency pub, with panelled walls, open fire and prints of the early 20thC canal scenes, in the heart of Little Venice. ④ **Clifton Little Venice** (No. 3), specializes in architectural salvage. You might find anything here from an 18thC gazebo to a couple of Doric columns. ⑤ One of the oldest roads in the area, **Warwick Avenue** was laid out in the 1840s and lined with grand well-spaced houses. ⑥ **Nos 2-16**. This handsome row has been attributed to the architect George Ledwell Taylor. ⑦ Through **Jason's Trip** (60 Blomfield Road, just off map) you can take the traditional 1906 narrowboat, the *Jason*, on a pretty excursion through Regent's Park and the Zoo to Camden Lock. ⑧ Overlooking the most picturesque stretch of canal, dotted with brightly painted houseboats, **Blomfield Road** and ⑨ **Maida Avenue** are lined with handsome 19thC white stucco houses. ⑩ **Grand Union Canal**, opened at the beginning of the 19thC and designed to link London to the Midlands at a time when the waterways formed the most efficient method of transport. It joins ⑪ the **Regent's Canal**, which runs eight miles through 12 locks to the Thames at Limehouse. ⑫ Among the well-known occupants of villas in **Delamere Terrace** were Victorian writer Sir Edmund Gosse, and Antarctic explorer Edmund Wilson. ⑬ **Canal office**, a former toll-house. ⑭ **London Waterbus Company** operates a service to the Zoo and Camden Lock from here. ⑮ **Little Venice**. Browning first compared the area to Venice, but the term was not coined until after the Second World War. Surrounded by busy thoroughfares, it is one of the least expected, prettiest parts of the capital, much loved by artists. ⑯ **Tow-paths**, tranquil places to stroll. ⑰ Before **Warwick Crescent** was pulled down and rebuilt in the 1960s, Robert Browning lived at No. 19. ⑱ **No. 2** was a hostel for musicians, where the short story writer Katherine Mansfield stayed in the early 1900s. ⑲ An old Celtic track and later Paddington's High Street, **Harrow Road** was completely redeveloped in the 1960s with the construction of ⑳ **Westway**.

The Bedford Estate

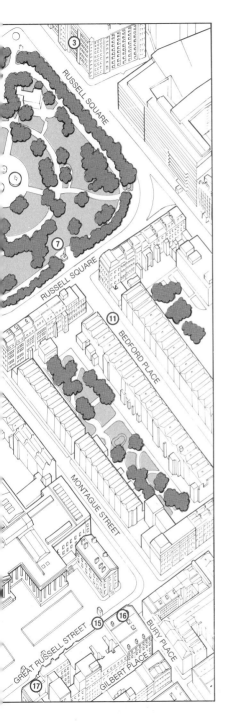

① **Torrington Square**, built by James Sim in 1821-5 on the 'field of forty footsteps', where two brothers fought a duel in the 1680s, killing each other, but leaving behind 40 footprints. ② London University's **School of Oriental and African Studies**. ③ Charles Fitzroy Doll's rambling red-brick and terracotta **Hotel Russell**. ④ **Russell Square** (1800), one of the largest squares on the Bedford Estate; favoured by 19thC lawyers. ⑤ **Malet Street**, now dominated by university buildings. ⑥ **Birkbeck College**, founded by Dr George Birkbeck in 1823 to provide degree courses for people with jobs. ⑦ **Bronze** by Sir Richard Westmacott of the 5th Duke of Bedford, Francis Russell (1809); the Dukes of Bedford owned estates in Bloomsbury and Covent Garden. ⑧ Although Ruskin thought **Gower Street** an architectural disaster, one resident, actress Sarah Siddons described 'the back of it' as 'most effectually in the country and delightfully pleasant'. ⑨ **London School of Hygiene and Tropical Medicine**. ⑩ Charles Holden's monolithic **Senate House** (1932) in Portland stone has a 210ft tower; it contains offices and the University's famous library. ⑪ **Bedford Place**, built by James Burton (1801-5) on the site of Southampton House (c1657). ⑫ **Bedford Square**. Most of the elegant brick houses in Bloomsbury's only intact Georgian square are now the offices of publishers and architects. The central houses on each side are decorated with stucco pediments and pilasters. ⑬ **Nos 34-36**, occupied since 1917 by the Architectural Association. ⑭ **The British Museum** founded in 1753 with a bequest of 50,000 items from physician and naturalist Sir Hans Sloane. The exhibits, ranging from zoological specimens to manuscripts, make the museum the largest and most varied in Britain. Here are the controversial Elgin Marbles, the Lycurgus Cup, Rosetta Stone, Mildenhall and Sutton Hoo Treasures and 2,000-year-old Lindow Man, contained in a huge neo-classical building by Robert Smirke (1838). The British Library's splendid semi-circular Reading Room (1857) has a massive blue iron dome and 25 miles of bookshelves. ⑮ '. . . a very handsome, large and well built street, graced with all the best buildings in Bloomsbury' was historian John Strype's description of **Great Russell Street**. ⑯ Bargain cashmere sweaters at **Westaway & Westaway** (No. 62). ⑰ Karl Marx and other scholars penned a line or two as they downed a pint at the **Museum Tavern** (No. 49).

47

▼68

High Holborn/Theobald's Road

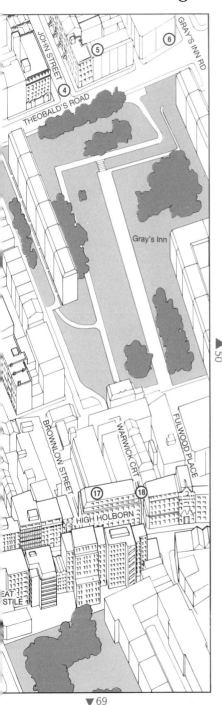

① **Lamb's Conduit Street**, named after a benevolent chorister at the Chapel Royal who restored the water conduit in 1577. ② **Great James Street**, a delightful and near-perfect 1720s street, lived in at various times by Swinburne, Dorothy L. Sayers, Leonard and Virginia Woolf, and T.S. Eliot. ③ **Cockpit Yard**, where cock-fighting took place in the 18thC. ④ **John Street**, a wide and gracious avenue with many original 18thC houses. ⑤ Disraeli was born at **22 Theobald's Road** in 1804; now Henekey's wine bar (**£**). ⑥ **The Yorkshire Grey** serves real ales brewed on the premises. ⑦ **The Central School of Art and Design** moved into this purpose-built edifice, by W.E. Riley, in 1908. Attached is the Jeannetta Cochrane Theatre, used by the students and named after a teacher at the school. ⑧ **Red Lion Square** was laid out in 1684 by Nicholas Barbon, despite the violent intervention of Gray's Inn lawyers who objected to the destruction of their local 'green belt'. ⑨ **No. 17** was the home of Dante Gabriel Rossetti and later of William Morris and Edward Burne-Jones. A bust of Bertrand Russell stands near the Conway Hall where he used to lecture (now a concert hall). ⑩ **Bedford Row**, unusually wide, was built c1700. It was well restored after bomb damage, though only two original houses (Nos 42 and 43) survive intact. ⑪ **High Holborn** is the main thoroughfare. The dusty office blocks of Holborn, solid and dependable, dominate this area despite its proximity to literary Bloomsbury and the mysterious Inns of Court; this is a place for work not play. ⑫ Perched high on the façade of the **National Westminster** Bank (No. 114) are statues of Edward I (the only one in London) and Edward VII (Richard Garb, 1902). ⑬ The vast late-Edwardian granite mansion of **Pearl Assurance**. ⑭ In front of State House (Nos 63-71) is a bronze, *Meridian*, by Barbara Hepworth. ⑮ **The Russian Shop** (No. 278) sells arts and crafts from all over the Soviet Union. ⑯ **Great Turnstile** (and **New Turnstile**) mark the stiles that kept cattle on Lincoln's Inn Fields (*see page 69*) when they were pastures. ⑰ **The HMSO Bookshop** (No. 49); no government publication is too obscure. ⑱ **The narrow lanes leading to Gray's Inn** (*see page 51*) serve to highlight the spaciousness and tranquillity of the gardens.

Gray's Inn Road

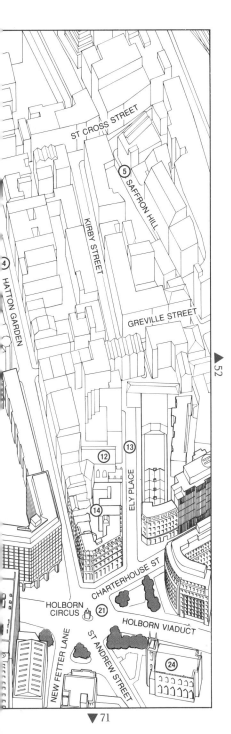

① **Gray's Inn Road**, once a link from the north to the City's markets. ② **Portpool Lane**, after Reginald le Grey's Purpoole Manor, which once occupied the site of Gray's Inn. ③ A bustling market in **Leather Lane**, held here since the 19thC, sells everything from fresh fruit and veg to jumpers and pot plants. ④ **Hatton Garden**, on the site of Hatton House, owned by Elizabeth I's Chancellor, Christopher Hatton. Today, the centre of London's diamond trade. ⑤ **Saffron Hill**, part of a 13thC garden, famous for its saffron, used to disguise rancid meat. By the 19thC the area was known as 'Thieves' Kitchen' as young criminals were put through their paces here. ⑥ **Verulam Buildings** (1803-11), named after Francis Bacon, 1st Lord Verulam, who laid out ⑦ **Gray's Inn Gardens** – better known as The Walks – Pepys's favourite spot for a stroll. ⑧ In **Gray's Inn Square**, ⑨ The Hall (1556) was scene of the first production of Shakespeare's *Comedy of Errors* (1594). Bombed in 1941, it was rebuilt by Sir Edward Maufe and still contains a remarkable late 16thC screen. ⑩ **St Alban the Martyr**, built by William Butterfield in the 1860s, and the centre of a Catholic Revival scandal. Rebuilt in 1945 by Adrian Scott. ⑪ The poet Chatterton committed suicide in a house on the **site of 39 Brooke Street**. ⑫ Roman Catholic **St Etheldreda's**, built in the late 13thC as a private chapel. ⑬ **Ely Place**, on the site of the Bishop of Ely's house; a Crown property, it is outside police jurisdiction. ⑭ Delightful 16thC **Ye Old Mitre** pub (Ely Court). ⑮ **Cittie of York**, 17thC wood-panelled pub with cubicles, where clients used to confer with their lawyers. ⑯ Half-timbered tobacconists, **John Brumfit** (No. 337). ⑰ and ⑱ **Holborn Bars**, where silver griffins mark the City boundary. ⑲ **Holborn**, 13thC route for the transport of goods to the City. ⑳ Dickens wrote *The Pickwick Papers* on the site of the vast Gothic red-brick and terracotta **Prudential Assurance building** by Alfred and Paul Waterhouse (No. 142). ㉑ **Statue of Prince Albert** raising his hat to the City of London by Charles Bacon (1874). ㉒ **London Silver Vaults** (53-64 Chancery Lane), warren of subterranean shops in the old Chancery Lane Safe Deposit Co. ㉓ Inn of Chancery, **Staple Inn**, founded in 1378. ㉔ **St Andrew's Church**, 10thC but much damaged and restored. Rebuilt sympathetically in the 1960s.

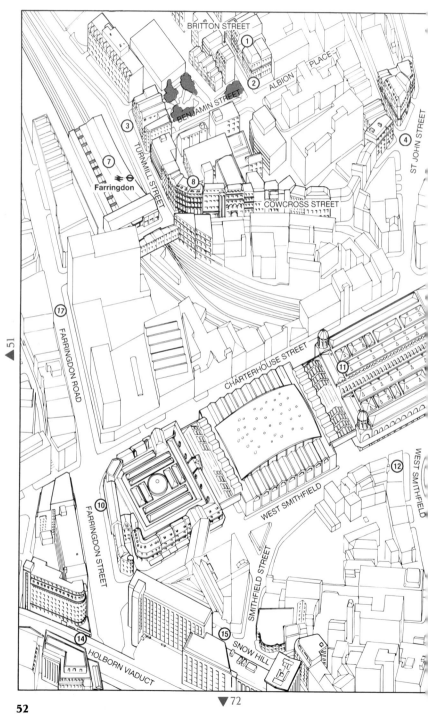

◀ 51

▼ 72

Smithfield

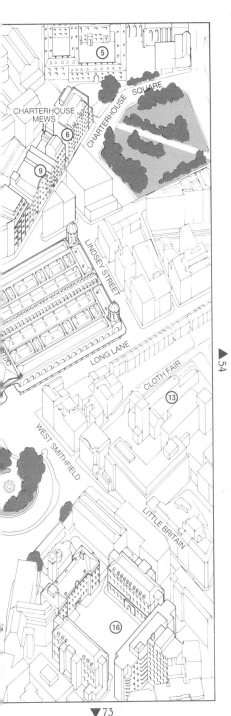

① 18thC **Albion Wireworks**, its exterior decorated with a model lion and unicorn, lit by gas jets for Queen Victoria's Golden Jubilee. ② Art nouveau façade of **Booth's Gin Distillery**, moved here from ③ **Turnmill Street**. ④ **St John's Street**, along which animals were driven on the last leg of their journey to market, once boasted 23 pubs. ⑤ **Charterhouse**, on the site of a 14thC Carthusian monastery founded by Sir Walter de Manny, Knight of Edward III. Built by royal master mason Henry Yevele and, after the Dissolution, bought by Thomas Howard, Duke of Norfolk. In the 17thC, Thomas Sutton converted it into a school for poor scholars and a hospice for gentlemen. The school moved to Surrey in 1872, and the building is now occupied by St Bartholomew's Medical School. ⑥ **Le Café du Marché** (22 Charterhouse Square), excellent French bistro in a converted warehouse (**££**). ⑦ **Farringdon Station** (1863), original terminus of the Metropolitan Line, the world's first underground railway. ⑧ The **Castle** (34 Cowcross Street), simple pub where the landlord has a pawnbroker's licence granted by George IV. ⑨ **The Fox and Anchor** (115 Charterhouse Street), friendly pub serving breakfast from 6.30 am. ⑩ **Smithfield Cellars**, wine bar and restaurant (**££**). ⑪ **Central Markets**. Smithfield refers to the 'smooth field', where markets, fairs, including Bartholomew Fair, and public executions were held. Sir Horace Jones's Italianate building opened in 1868. Still London's main meat market; not for the squeamish. ⑫ City slickers rub shoulders with meat market workers in the **Bishop's Finger** (9-10 West Smithfield). ⑬ **St Bartholomew the Great**, one of the City's oldest and most memorable churches, was part of a 12thC priory founded by Rahere, Henry I's court jester. It has an impressive nave and 16thC half-timbered gatehouse. Restored by Sir Aston Webb in the late 19thC. ⑭ Designed to link Holborn to Newgate (now Farringdon) Street, **Holborn Viaduct** (1863-9) was the costly but impressive achievement of City Surveyor William Heywood. This ornate bridge, the longest in a series, is decorated with bronze statues representing Victorian virtues. ⑮ **Snow Hill**, notorious for gangs who forced elderly women into barrels and rolled them down the hill. ⑯ **St Bartholomew's Hospital**, better known as Bart's, was also founded by Rahere. Spared during the Dissolution, it was rebuilt in the 18thC by James Gibbs, and is now one of London's most important teaching hospitals. ⑰ **Quality Chop House** (No. 94, off map), a 19thC chop house authentically restored; simple, good food, animated despite the uncomfy seats (**££**).

▲ 54

▼ 73

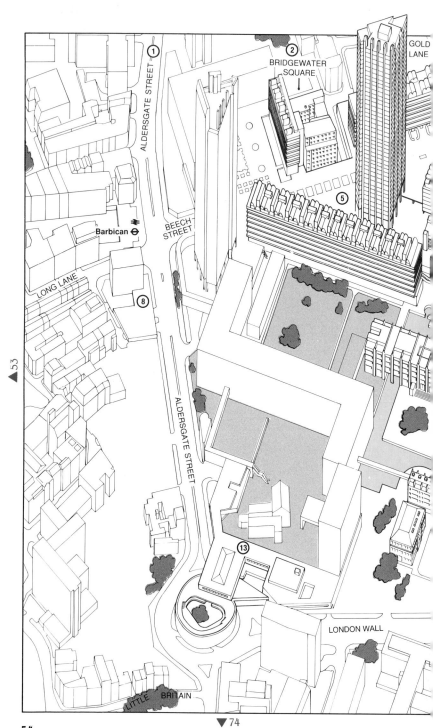

The Barbican

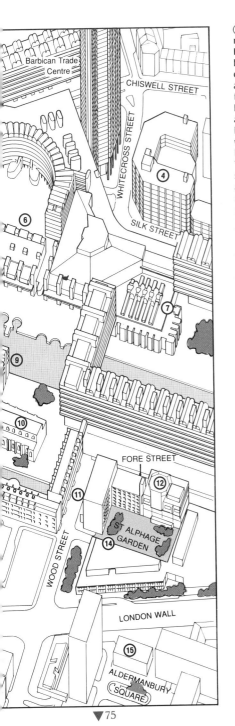

① According to James Howell in the mid-17thC, 'Aldersgate resembleth an Italian street more than any other in London by reason of the spaciousness and uniformity of buildings'. It was completely redeveloped after the Blitz. ② **Bridgewater Square**, on the site of a house built for Thomas Wriothesley, Garter King of Arms from 1504, but later acquired by the Earls of Bridgewater. The house burned down in the 17thC, and the site was developed by Wren. ③ **Golden Lane**, home of the Fortune Theatre (1660-1) and Thomas Killigrew's school for actors, The Nursery. ④ Although beer has not been brewed at **Whitbread's Brewery** (Chiswell Street) since the mid-1970s, the buildings have been preserved. ⑤ One of London's most controversial examples of post-war architecture, **The Barbican** was designed by Chamberlin, Powell & Bon, and intended to be the residential and cultural core of the City. Concrete towers, linked by high walkways, contain apartments, shops and schools, as well as ⑥ the **Barbican Arts and Conference Centre**. Covering 20 confusing acres (follow the yellow lines), the centre houses the London Symphony Orchestra's concert hall, the Royal Shakespeare Company's two theatres, an art gallery and three cinemas. ⑦ **Guildhall School of Music and Drama**. Founded as a music school in 1880, drama was introduced in 1935, and it moved here in 1977. ⑧ **London Salvage Corps**, established in 1866 to protect insured property from fire damage. ⑨ **City of London School for Girls**. ⑩ A church has stood on the site of blackened **St Giles Cripplegate** since the 11thC. It was devastated in World War II, and restored in the 1950s by Godfrey Allan. John Milton is buried in the churchyard. ⑪ Site of **Cripplegate**, one of the Roman city gates. The name probably derives from the Anglo-Saxon *crepel*, meaning covered way. Edmund the Martyr's body was carried through the gate in the 11thC and held responsible for the miraculous cure of cripples. ⑫ Sir Basil Spence's **Salters' Hall** (1976). ⑬ The well-organized **Museum of London** charts the social history of the city from prehistory to the present. Exhibits range from Roman finds to the Lord Mayor's Ceremonial Coach. (Closed Mon.) ⑭ A section of the medieval city wall stands in **St Alphage Garden**, churchyard of the now vanished St Alphage London Wall. ⑮ In the garden of Brewers' Hall is a charming **bronze sculpture** entitled *The Gardener* by Karin Jonzen (1971).

▼75

Marble Arch

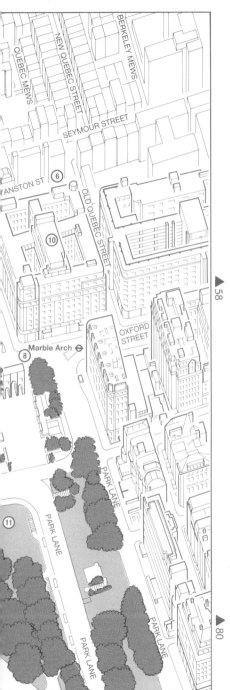

① The **West London Synagogue**, built in 1870. ② **Connaught Square** (1820s) is a delightful backwater which marks the start of the attractive squares and streets of Hyde Park Estate (off map) once known as Tyburnia. ③ Characterless **Edgware Road** lies along Watling Street, the Roman highway to St Albans, and is still a main route in and out of town. ④ **Al-Medina** (No. 7). Busy self-service café/restaurant offering good samosas, felafel, kebabs and the like (**£**). ⑤ **Maroush** (No. 21) also reflects the strong Middle-Eastern influence in this area and serves tasty Lebanese food (**££**). ⑥ The Edwardian **Church of the Annunciation**. ⑦ Like its continuation, Oxford Street, **Bayswater Road** was an important Roman road. After the rigours of the former, the latter, running the length of the park, seems almost peaceful. It is lined, in the main, with dignified 19thC buildings, and on Sundays lurid paintings are offered for sale along its parkside railings. ⑧ Like Constitution Arch at Hyde Park Corner, **Marble Arch** is marooned on a traffic island, hardly noticed by harrassed car drivers, hardly accessible to pedestrians. Like Admiralty Arch, only royalty (and the King's Troop, Royal Horse Artillery) may pass through its central gates. Designed by John Nash, it stood in front of Buckingham Palace from 1827, but moved here in 1851, and was marooned in 1908. Nearby a plaque marks the site of the infamous Tyburn gallows where, until their removal to Newgate (*see page 73*) in 1783, mass public hangings, attracting vast and clamorous crowds who had been given a celebratory day off work, were carried out. ⑨ At the **Tyburn Convent** (8 Hyde Park Place) an order of Roman Catholic nuns perpetuate the memory, in their constant prayers, of the 105 Catholic martyrs who died at Tyburn. ⑩ The **Cumberland**, vast, conventional hotel near the Odeon cinema. ⑪ If you have an orange box and something to say (that is not obscene, or blasphemous or an incitement to breach the peace) then you can do so by law at **Speaker's Corner** on a Sunday. Alternatively join the hecklers, or just watch the fun.

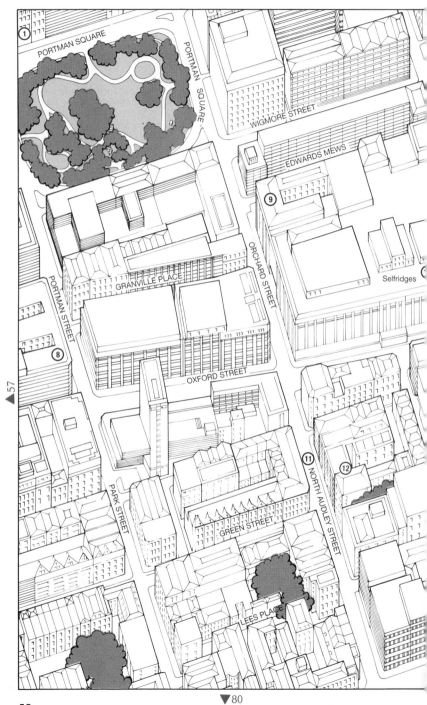

Selfridges

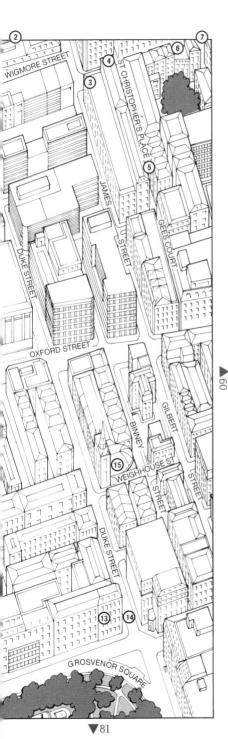

① **Home House** (20 Portman Square), one of only two surviving Robert Adam mansions in central London (1773-7), has a lovely, delicately wrought interior. ② Just to the north in Manchester Square (off map) is the **Wallace Collection**. London's most seductive art museum, it contains the works of art collected by the Hertford family in the 18th and 19thCs. Amongst many European masterpieces it includes perhaps the finest collection of French art, furniture and *objets d'art* outside France, all in the family's palatial town house, left to the nation in 1897. ③ **Jane Packer** (56 James Street). Floral nostalgia from Fergie's wedding-day florist. ④ The **Pontefract Castle**, an exuberantly decorated free house. ⑤ Unexpectedly narrow and prettified, **St Christopher's Place** and **Gees Court** are lined with a mix of pricey boutiques and rather twee restaurants. ⑥ Capt. Benson and Mr Dickson combined to open **Bendicks**, the chocolate makers, after the First World War (No. 55). ⑦ **John Bell & Croyden** (No. 54), 'a hypochondriac's heaven', sells everything from aspirins to blood pressure kits and surgeons' knives. ⑧ The huge but unobtrusive **Mount Royal Hotel**. ⑨ The **Selfridge Hotel**, prestigious member of the Thistle chain. ⑩ **Selfridges**. Built by American magnate Gordon Selfridge (1907-28) this is London's most magnificent store, though it has always lacked the glamour of Harrods. Inside, it has everything, including magical window displays at Christmas. ⑪ Like nearby Green Street and pretty Lees Place, **North Audley Street** is part of the Grosvenor Estate (*see page 81*). It recalls Sir Hugh Audley, the man from whom the Grosvenor acres originally descended via a propitious marriage. Only Nos 11 and 12, designed by Edward Shepherd, remain from the 18thC. ⑫ **St Mark** (closed) has an impressively tall Greek portico. ⑬ The **London Marriott Hotel**. ⑭ Long-established shops in **Duke Street** are: **H.R. Higgins** (No. 79), purveyors of coffee and tea in wood-panelled premises; **A. Nelson & Co** (No. 73), homoeopathic pharmacy; and **Allans** (Nos 56-58), a fabric shop where you can buy silks costing up to £700 a yard. ⑮ Alfred Waterhouse's **Ukrainian Catholic Cathedral** (1889-91).

Oxford Street/Hanover Square

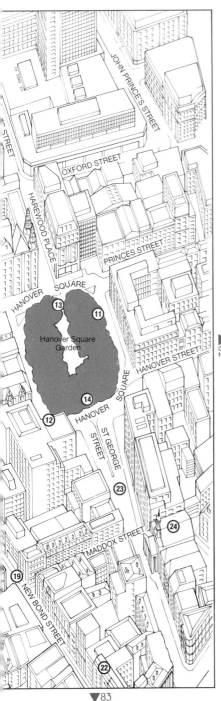

① On a pretty island site is **St Peter's Church** (1721-4, James Gibbs); much of the original decoration has been removed or painted over. ② **Cavendish Square** (1717), first of the great northward developments by the Cavendish family. ③ Prime Minister Asquith lived at **No. 20** from 1895 to 1908. ④ A glimpse of **Stratford Place**, with the imposing façade of the Oriental Club at its end, revives the spirit after the brashness of Oxford Street. The revamped **Debenhams** ⑤ and model department store, **John Lewis**, ⑥ dominate this street which is otherwise devoted to chain-store shopping. ⑦ Notice the wrought-iron arch erected by Angelo Sedley in 1873 to promote his furniture business, an early example of advertising. ⑧ **South Molton Street**, now a chic pedestrian precinct, was once called Poverty Lane. William Blake lived in penury at No. 17; at No. 46 is **Widow Applebaum's**, Jewish wine bar and deli (**£**); at Nos 23-27 is **Browns**, high-profile boutique. ⑨ **Gray's Market** (1-7 Davies Mews and 58 Davies Street). Huge and bewildering stock of antiques in two covered markets. ⑩ **Chicago Pizza Pie Factory** (No. 17), Bob Payton's original all-American pizzeria (**£**). ⑪ Few of the original houses in **Hanover Square** remain but ⑫ **No. 24**, a tall pretty brick house, squeezed by modern buildings gives an idea of how it once looked. To the north of the square is ⑬, a restored **cabman's shelter** resembling a miniature cricket pavilion, and to the south, opposite, ⑭ a huge **bronze of William Pitt the Younger** by Chantrey (1831), which proved too solid for the radicals who tried to pull it down. ⑮ Literary gentleman's club, the **Savile**, with a prettily ornate interior. ⑯ Traditional luxury, complete discretion and distinguished faces are assured at **Claridge's** hotel. ⑰ **Ikeda** (No. 30), expensive Japanese restaurant; sushi is best (**£££**). ⑱ **No. 25**, Handel's home for over 30 years until his death in 1759. ⑲ Although architecturally unremarkable, **Bond Street** has, since Georgian times, been famous for its luxury shops. If you have to ask the price, you can't afford it. Shops in this stretch (New Bond Street) include ⑳ the department store **Fenwicks** (No. 63), ㉑ **Giorgio Armani** at No. 123, ㉒ **Sotheby's**, the auctioneers, at Nos 34-35, and **Asprey**, the famous jewellers, goldsmiths and silversmiths at No. 165 (*see page 85*). ㉓ Funnel-shaped **St George Street** with its fine houses (particularly No. 15) narrows at ㉔ **St George's Church** (1721-4, John James). London's first porticoed church, now unfortunately marred by grime.

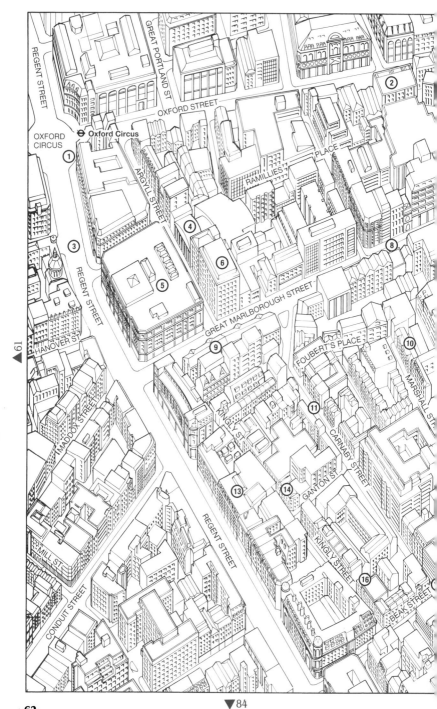

REGENT STREET

GREAT PORTLAND ST

OXFORD STREET

Oxford Circus

OXFORD CIRCUS

①

ARGYLL STREET

RAMILLIES PLACE

②

③

REGENT STREET

④

⑥

⑤

⑧

GREAT MARLBOROUGH STREET

FOUBERT'S PLACE

HANOVER ST

⑨

KINGLY ST

⑩

MARSHALL ST

⑪

CARNABY STREET

MADDOX STREET

⑬

⑭

GANTON ST

MILL ST

CONDUIT STREET

REGENT STREET

KINGLY STREET

⑯

BEAK STREET

19

62

▼84

Regent Street

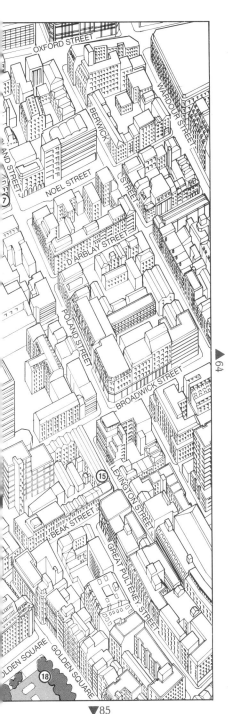

① **Oxford Circus**, with four identical quadrants designed by Sir Henry Tanner (1913-28). ② Site of the 18thC **Pantheon**, sumptuously decorated and known as the 'winter Ranelagh', where amusements included masquerades, assemblies and concerts. Marks and Spencer now occupies the site. ③ Nash's grand, sweeping **Regent Street** (1817-23); built as part of an ambitious scheme for the Prince Regent, linking Regent's Park to Carlton House (*see page 109*). The most fashionable shops opened in the colonnaded Quadrant, redesigned in 1916. The famous Christmas lights were first switched on in 1954. ④ **London Palladium** (1910) – designed as a luxurious music-hall by Frank Matcham for Walter Gibbons – has been associated with popular entertainment ever since.
⑤ **Dickins & Jones**, fashion and beauty store. ⑥ Black granite, with gilt floral motives, **Palladium House** was designed by American architect Raymond Hood in 1928. ⑦ **Coach and Horses**, 18thC coaching inn on the old Bath road. ⑧ **Great Marlborough Street** commemorates the Duke of Marlborough's victory at Blenheim. ⑨ **Liberty**, department store, set up to import Oriental goods, and famous for its printed fabrics and mock-Tudor building. ⑩ **Cranks** (No. 8), counter-service restaurant for the health-conscious (**£**). ⑪ Seedy relic of the 'swinging sixties', **Carnaby Street** has had a facelift in recent years, but remains an anachronism. ⑫ **Craftsmen Potters Shop** (7 Marshall Street), where the pottery ranges from rustic mugs to full-blown sculptures. ⑬ Reputedly 'the finest toyshop in the world', **Hamleys** boasts six floors, crammed with games, cars, trains, models, robots, animals, dolls and endless other toys. ⑭ **Harry's** (No. 19) serves breakfast to night owls from 10 pm to 9 am. ⑮ **Andrew Edmunds** runs his own charming, simple Wine Bar & Restaurant (No. 46; **££**) with panache. He also owns the fusty print shop next door. ⑯ Lively wine bar and brasserie, **Shampers** (No. 4; **£**). ⑰ **Beak Street**, the major part of which was built in the late 17thC by Thomas Beak, Messenger to Queen Mary. ⑱ **Golden Square**, built between 1670 and the 1700s on Gelding's Close and a corruption of the name. A fashionable address in the early 18thC, it was then occupied by foreign legations and declined in the 19thC. Later in the century woollen merchants moved in, and today many of the buildings are let to film-makers.

▶ 64

▼85

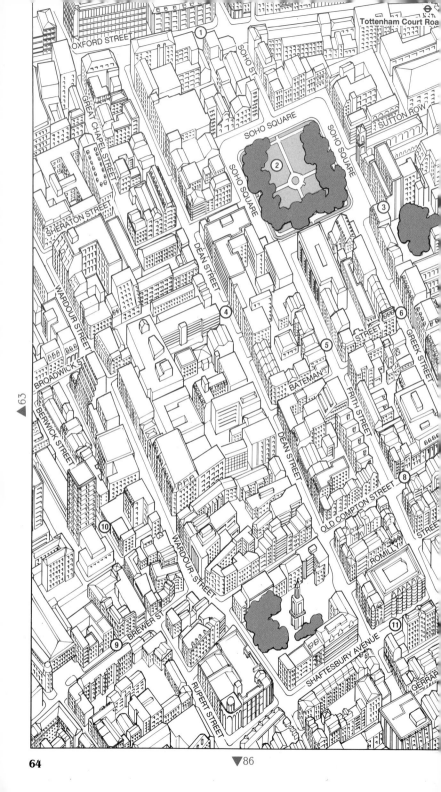

Soho

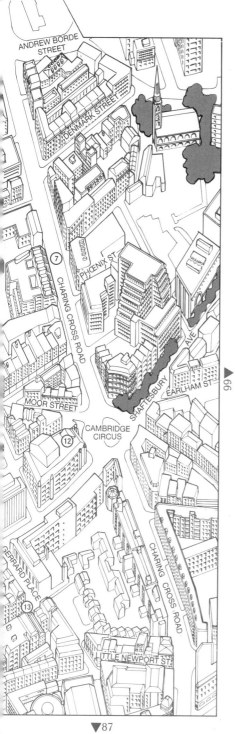

① **Oxford Street**, London's principal shopping street, has been a road since Roman times. ② Melancholy **Soho Square**, laid out in the 1680s, but greatly altered. Notice the French Protestant Church: the French, particularly exiled Huguenots, were the first wave of foreigners to settle in Soho. They were soon followed by many others, giving this endearing area its distinctive villagey yet cosmopolitan flavour. In the late 19thC began its reputation for food (undimmed) and for sleaze (still very much a part, but now in check). ③ The **House of St Barnabas** (1746), a lone reminder of Soho's aristocratic beginnings, with a magnificent 1750s rococo interior (open Wed & Thur). Now a hostel for homeless women. ④ In **Dean Street**, media folk hang out at the **Groucho Club** (No. 44), diners at **Leoni's Quo Vadis** (Nos 26-29; **£££**) can ask to see the rooms where Karl Marx and family lived in disordered poverty. **Pizza Express** (live jazz) is at No. 10 (**£**); **Red Fort** (good Indian food) at No. 77 (**££**). ⑤ In **Frith Street** the child Mozart stayed at No. 20; John Logie Baird first demonstrated television above **Bahn Thai** (No. 21a; **££**); and essayist William Hazlitt died at No. 6, now **Hazlitt's**, a charming small hotel. **Ronnie Scott's** jazz club is at No. 47; **Alastair Little** feeds the media in his eponymous restaurant at No. 49 (**£££**); Soho's Italian population congregate at the **Bar Italia** (No. 22), with the happening crowd swelling the crowds after hours (open 23 hours a day). **Jimmy's** (very cheap Greek) is next door at No. 23 (**£**). ⑥ In **Greek Street**, **L'Escargot** (opened in 1900; motto 'slow but sure') is enjoying its third incarnation as a fashionable restaurant (No. 48; **£££**); the **Gay Hussar** still packs them in for its wild cherry soup after 35 years (No. 2; **£££**); and old-timer **Maison Bertaux** still serves delectable pastries (No. 28). ⑦ **Charing Cross Road** is lined with bookshops. ⑧ In **Old Compton Street**, **Pollo's** (No. 20) is a cheap, chaotic **Italian café** (**£**), while **Café Bohème** packs them in until 3 am. Don't miss **Patisserie Valerie** (No. 44) or Italian delicatessen **Camisa** (No. 61). A knot of similar continental provision stores, as well as fishmonger **Richards** can be found in ⑨ **Brewer Street**, plus the up-market part of ⑩ jolly **Berwick Street Market**. ⑪ **Shaftesbury Avenue**, London's theatreland, culminates at Cambridge Circus with ⑫ the restored **Palace Theatre**. ⑬ **Gerrard Street**, pedestrian-only heart of Chinatown. Amazing supermarkets and amusing restaurants abound. Notable are: **New World** (especially for *dim sum*; No 1 Gerrard Place; **££**); **Dragon Gate** (No. 7; **£**); and **London Chinatown** (No. 27; **££**).

ST GILES HIGH STREET

SHAFTESBURY AVENUE

NEAL STREET

NEAL'S YARD

ENDELL STREET

MONMOUTH STREET

EARLHAM STREET

SEVEN DIALS

SHELTON STREET

MERCER STREET

Covent Garden

LONG ACRE

UPPER ST MARTIN'S LANE

FLORAL STREET

JAMES STREET

KING STREET

GARRICK STREET

Leicester Square

65

66

▼ 88

Covent Garden

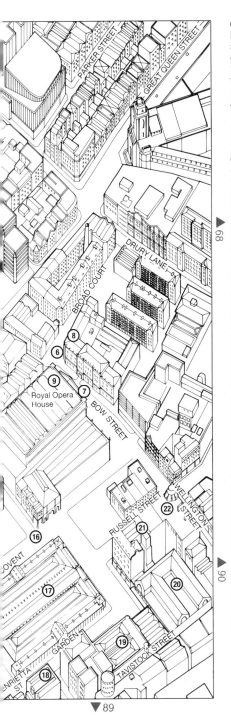

① Erstwhile Mélange (No. 59) has become **Mars**, but otherwise not much has changed – still *'cuisine libre'* and crazy 'vandalized' décor (**£££**). ② **Mon Plaisir** (No. 21), archetypical French bistro (**££**). ③ An ingenious water-clock heralds the entrance to higgledy-piggledy wholefood enclave, **Neal's Yard**. ④ At **Seven Dials** the original sundial monument has recently been replaced. It was removed in 1773 in a vain attempt to disperse lurking criminals. ⑤ Fringe theatre, the **Donmar Warehouse** (41 Earlham Street). ⑥ Enzo Plazotta's bronze dancer sits at the entrance to contemplative **Broad Court** and the budget **Fielding Hotel**. ⑦ The novelist Henry Fielding lived in **Bow Street** and formed forerunners to the police, the Bow Street Runners when a magistrate at ⑧ the **Courts** in 1749. ⑨ Controversial plans to extend the **Royal Opera House** (dull exterior, wonderful auditorium; E.M. Barry 1858) will mean a much-postponed closure for two years in 1997. ⑩ **Edward Stanford** (Nos 13-14) has the world's largest collection of maps and travel books. ⑪ The **Garrick Club** (No. 15). ⑫ **The Ivy** (1 West Street, obscured; **£££**), bygone theatrical restaurant, brought back to life with great success by the Caprice team. ⑬ **The Lamb and Flag**, a 300-year-old pub with a rough past – it used to be called the Bucket of Blood. ⑭ **The Calabash** in the **Africa Centre** (No. 38) for hearty African food (**£**). ⑮ **St Paul's** (1631). Inigo Jones's 'handsomest barn in England' is known as the actors' church, and has wall plaques commemorating thespians from 1680 to the present day. It is all that remains of his great residential square, the first in London, commissioned by the Earl of Bedford. ⑯ Originally a convent garden, Jones's square, always known as the **Piazza** because of its Italianate design, lost its fashionable status when a fruit and vegetable market flourished in its midst. In the 19thC proper market halls were built, starting with ⑰ **Central Market**. When the famous market with its Cockney dawn chorus left for Nine Elms in 1974, the Piazza took on new life as an up-market shopping enclave. Since then street entertainment and swarms of young people have kept Covent Garden humming. ⑱ **Boulestin** (No. 1a), grand French restaurant (**£££**). ⑲ Cheap and cheerful stalls in **Jubilee Hall**. ⑳ **London Transport Museum**, covering the history of public transport in London; much livelier than it sounds. ㉑ **Boswell's Coffee House** (No. 8), where Boswell was introduced to Dr Johnson (it was a bookshop at the time). ㉒ **Theatre Museum**. A tribute to the British stage.

▲48

GATE STREET

⊖ Holborn

① KINGSWAY

②

REMNANT STREET

③ LINCOLN'S INN FIELDS

④

⑥

⑦ PORTSMOUTH STREET

KINGSWAY

⑩

▲67

KEMBLE STREET

KEAN STREET

⑫

HOUGHTON STREET

⑬ DRURY LANE

⑭

⑯

RUSSELL STREET

TAVISTOCK STREET

⑮

ALDWYCH

⑱

⑲

▼90

Lincoln's Inn Fields

① **Kingsway**, the main road in the Victorians' final improvement scheme for London (1905). ② **Ship Tavern**, 16thC pub with a priest's hole; haunt of the legal fraternity. ③ **The Soane Museum**, found in three houses that belonged to eccentric architect Sir John Soane, who assembled a miscellany of objects from the sarcophagus of Seti I to Hogarth's *The Rake's Progress* (closed Sun & Mon). ④ **Lincoln's Inn Fields**, one of London's largest squares, laid out on common land. The mid-17thC brick houses, built by developer William Newton, are now mostly lawyers' chambers. ⑤ One of the four Inns of Court, **Lincoln's Inn** was founded in the 14thC and retains its collegiate atmosphere. ⑥ A handsome building with wreathed Ionic pilasters, **Lindsey House** is probably by Inigo Jones. ⑦ **Dickens's Old Curiosity Shop** selling 'antiques and souvenirs' was already 275 years old when he knew it, and has been unchanged since 1700. ⑧ Charles Barry's **Royal College of Surgeons**, which houses the remarkable collection of 18thC surgeon and scientist, John Hunter. ⑨ **Portugal Street**, where in 1661 Sir William D'Avenant opened the Lincoln's Inn Fields Theatre in a converted tennis-court. ⑩ **Royalty Theatre**, built by Bertie Crewe in 1911 as a rival to Covent Garden. ⑪ G.E. Street's 19thC Gothic pile, the **Royal Courts of Justice** or Law Courts, built to amalgamate all the superior civil courts. ⑫ **London School of Economics and Political Science**. ⑬ **Drury Lane**, a fashionable address in the 16th and 17thC, which degenerated into an area notorious for its drunken brawls. ⑭ Benjamin Wyatt's **Theatre Royal Drury Lane** (1811-12) is the fourth on the site. A theatre was first built in 1663 for the King's Company; buildings by Wren and Henry Holland followed. The ghost of a man found murdered in the 19thC allegedly haunts the circle. ⑮ W.G.R. Sprague's **Aldwych Theatre** (1905), home of the Royal Shakespeare Company 1960-82. ⑯ King Alfred endowed the defeated Danes with the land now occupied by the **Aldwych**. ⑰ Wren's **St Clement Danes**, with its Portland stone tower and open spire, topped by a dome and turret by James Gibbs (1719). ⑱ **Waldorf Hotel**, famous for its tea dances. ⑲ **Bush House** (1923-35), planned as a trade centre and now home of the BBC World Service. ⑳ A. Marshall Mackenzie's *beaux-arts* **Australia House**. ㉑ **Statue of Gladstone**, with four allegorical figures at its base (1905), by Sir William Hamo Thornycroft.

▲49

LINCOLN'S INN FIELDS

NEW SQUARE

SERLE STREET

PORTUGAL STREET

CAREY STREET

STRAND

▶70

Fleet Street

① The heart of legal London, **Chancery Lane** is so called because Henry III granted the land to his Lord Chancellor in the 13thC. ② **White Horse**, old coaching inn, where a well-dressed ghost makes nocturnal forays into the cellar. ③ **Lincoln's Inn Chapel** (1619-23) boasts some fine box pews and stained glass. ④ **Printer's Devil**, pub which takes its name from the colloquial term for a printer's apprentice. ⑤ **Ede and Ravenscroft** (No. 93), legal robe-makers, where aspiring barristers also buy their made-to-measure horsehair wigs. ⑥ The saying 'in **Carey Street**' to describe a bankrupt dates from the time when the bankruptcy courts were here. ⑦ Lewis Vulliamy's **Law Society** (1831), with additions by Charles Holden (1902). ⑧ Mock Tudor **Public Record Office** (1851-66) contains records dating back to the Norman Conquest. The museum (open Mon-Fri), on the site of the Rolls Chapel, displays the *Domesday Book*, Guy Fawkes's confession and Shakespeare's will. ⑨ **Dr Johnson's House** (17 Gough Square), where the great man lived 1749-59 and compiled his Dictionary in the attic. ⑩ **Royal Courts of Justice** (*see page 69*). ⑪ John Shaw's Gothic Revival **St Dunstan-in-the-West** (1829-33), decorated with a clock (incorporating two figures that strike a bell), Lutyens' memorial to Lord Northcliffe and a statue of Elizabeth I from Ludgate. ⑫ **Ye Olde Cheshire Cheese**, rambling pub above the crypt of Whitefriars Monastery. ⑬ **Fleet Street's** association with the printing industry dates back to Caxton. It was once lined with booksellers, printers and binders, and until recently all London's major newspapers had their offices in or around 'The Street'. A technological revolution in the 1980s resulted in the computerization of much of the papers' production and a mass exodus of papers from Fleet Street to Docklands and other areas. ⑭ **El Vino's**, a male stronghold despite the 1982 court ruling that women should be served drinks at the bar. ⑮ **Temple Bar**, 19thC memorial designed by Sir Horace Jones. ⑯ **Ye Olde Cock Tavern**. ⑰ Every kind of tea, from Assam to Yunnan, is stocked by **R. Twining and Co.** (No. 216). ⑱ Chillingly romantic **Temple Church**, 12thC with later additions, is circular with a rib-vaulted porch and marble effigies of the Knights Templar. ⑲ Site of the Carmelite **Whitefriars Priory** founded in the mid-13thC. ⑳ **Inner Temple Hall** and ㉑ **Library** by Sir Hubert Worthington.

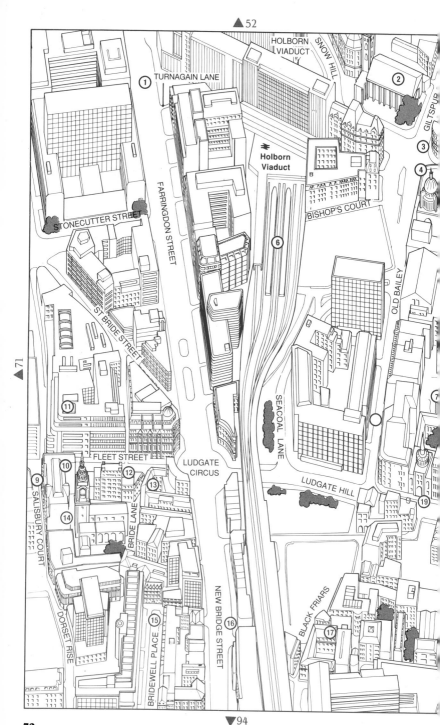

▲52

THE CITY

① TURNAGAIN LANE

HOLBORN VIADUCT

SNOW HILL

②

GILTSPUR

③

④

Holborn
Viaduct

BISHOP'S COURT

STONECUTTER STREET

FARRINGDON STREET

⑥

OLD BAILEY

ST BRIDE STREET

▲71

SEACOAL LANE

⑦

⑪

FLEET STREET

LUDGATE
CIRCUS

LUDGATE HILL

⑩

⑨

⑫

⑬

SALISBURY COURT

BRIDE LANE

⑭

⑲

NEW BRIDGE STREET

DORSET RISE

BLACK FRIARS

⑮

⑯

⑰

BRIDEWELL PLACE

▼94

Ludgate Hill

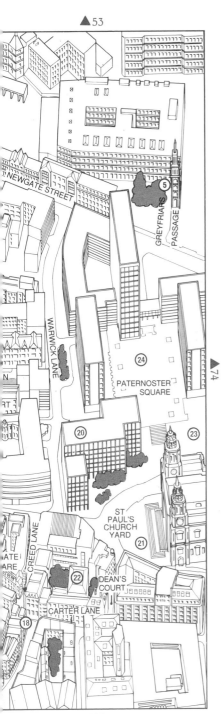

① **Turnagain Lane** once led to the Fleet River (*see page 95*); since no bridge existed there, you had to turn back. ② **St Sepulchre**, last ecclesiastical victim of the Great Fire, which died out just beyond. ③ **Viaduct Tavern** (1869) has a beautiful Victorian interior. The cellars are former Newgate prison cells; that grisly establishment was in its time ravaged by gaol fever, ransacked by the Gordon Rioters, and witness to highly popular public hangings. ④ **Old Bailey** (Central Criminal Court), stage for famous trials since 1539. The present building dates from 1900 (public admitted). ⑤ The elegant three-stage tower is all that remains of Wren's **Christ Church Greyfriars**, destroyed in the Blitz. ⑥ **Site of Fleet Prison**. A barbarous place, it closed in 1842. ⑦ A row of 17thC canons' houses and a little garden make **Amen Court** a haven. ⑧ **Stationers' Hall**, dating from 1667, with a later façade. ⑨ Samuel Pepys was born in a house in **Salisbury Court**. ⑩ Lutyens's sympathetic headquarters for **Reuters** (No. 85; 1935) stands opposite ⑪ the dominating black glass and chrome **ex-Daily Express building** (1932), with its wonderfully extravagant art deco entrance hall. ⑫ **Old Bell Inn**, built by Wren to succour the builders of St Bride. ⑬ **Punch Tavern**, where *Punch* magazine was conceived in 1841. ⑭ Hemmed in yet aloof, Wren's **St Bride** has a remarkable spire like an extended telescope and has been the model for wedding cakes ever since a Fleet Street pastry cook, Mr Rich, took to copying it in the 18thC. An exhibition in the crypt reveals the intriguing history of the site. ⑮ **Bridewell Place** commemorates Henry VIII's Bridewell Palace, which later became a prison. The demure **prison offices** (1805) remain at ⑯ No. 14. ⑰ **Apothecaries' Hall**, its fine interior virtually unchanged since 1688. ⑱ **Carter Lane**, once a main thoroughfare, has retained its historic scale in an engulfing sea of oversize commercial building. ⑲ Wren's **St Martin Ludgate** is a simple foil to his masterpiece, St Paul's; regrettably, the view of the cathedral from here is impaired by the 1960s mistake, ⑳ **Juxon House**. ㉑ The **west entrance of St Paul's** (*see page 75*) with a dour and dumpy statue of Queen Anne in front. ㉒ The **Deanery** and ㉓ **Chapter House** are also by Wren, the latter marooned by the inept post-war rebuilding around ㉔ **Paternoster Square**, now undergoing redevelopment.

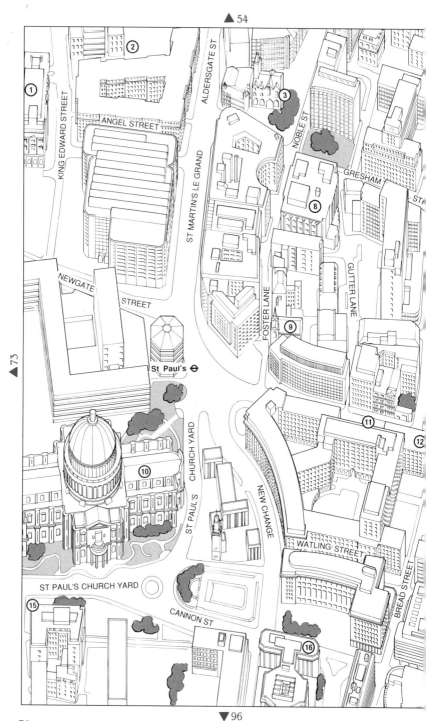

ANGEL STREET

KING EDWARD STREET

ALDERSGATE ST

ST MARTIN'S LE GRAND

NOBLE ST

GRESHAM ST

NEWGATE STREET

FOSTER LANE

GUTTER LANE

St Paul's ⊖

ST PAUL'S CHURCH YARD

NEW CHANGE

WATLING STREET

BREAD STREET

ST PAUL'S CHURCH YARD

CANNON ST

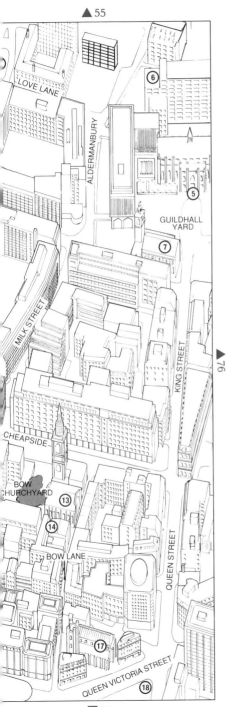

① London's head post office. Upstairs: a riot of colour in the **National Postal Museum**; underground: the unique post office railway linking the capital's sorting offices. ② **Postman's Park**, aptly named oasis with a wall of heart-rending plaques dedicated to selfless late-Victorian heroes and heroines. ③ **St Anne and St Agnes**, a Wren church in appealing domestic style. ④ **St Alban's** church tower, now an office, sole pre-war survivor in Wood Street of the Blitz. ⑤ **Guildhall**, powerhouse of the Corporation of the City of London for 1000 years. The present building dates from the 15thC with an unusual façade and a vast medieval crypt. The bland modern west wing ⑥ houses the **Guildhall Library** (unparalleled collection of documents on London) and the **Clockmakers' Company Museum**. ⑦ Wren's **St Lawrence Jewry**, with bold Corinthian east front. ⑧ **Goldsmiths' Hall** has a massive early 19thC exterior and a suitably rich interior (for details of 'open' days and all other information about the City tel: 260 1456). ⑨ **St Vedast-alias-Foster** has a late-Wren (1694) baroque steeple. ⑩ Born of the Great Fire of 1666, Sir Christopher Wren's masterpiece, **St Paul's Cathedral** miraculously survived the capital's second inferno, the Blitz. Ironically, the cathedral's impact has since then been spoiled by ill-considered post-war development. Wren's remarkable output in the three decades which followed the Great Fire totalled 53 City churches, all displaying his rational, yet deeply felt approach to religion; 23 survive today. '. . . if you seek his monument look around you' reads his epitaph under the cathedral's huge dome. There is much to see, not least the famous Whispering Gallery. ⑪ The merchandise in the medieval market of **Cheapside** was organized into individual lanes: hence Bread, Milk, Wood, Goldsmith and Friday (fish) Streets. ⑫ **Le Poulbot** (No. 45), once *the* City restaurant, has been sold by its well-known owners, the Roux brothers (though they have kept their flagship, The Gavroche (see page 81), and may by now be in new hands.(**£££**). ⑬ Anyone living within the sound of Bow Bells, which ring out from Wren's marvellous steeple of **St Mary-le-Bow**, can call themselves a true Cockney. ⑭ **Bow Wine Vaults** (10 Bow Churchyard), wine merchant and wine bar – one of the City's old favourites. ⑮ **City Information Centre**. ⑯ **Bracken House** (Sir Albert Richardson, 1956), the first post-war building to be listed. ⑰ Wren's **St Mary Aldermary**. ⑱ **Sweetings** (No. 39). Fish, shellfish and sandwiches; unchanged since 1830 (**££**).

Bank of England

① **Basinghall Street**, where onlookers used to stare in incredulity at Sir Walter Raleigh smoking a pipe. ② **The Institute of Chartered Accountants**, by John Belcher, 1889. ③ **Austin Friars** recalls the powerful Augustinian monastery which stood here from 1253. ④ The surviving Wren tower of **St Olave Jewry** is now part of an office complex. ⑤ **Old Jewry** was the medieval home of the City's Jewish merchants. Driven out by Edward I, they returned in the 17thC. ⑥ Terraced Adam houses in **Frederick's Place**: a little spot of orderliness amid the jungle. ⑦ Wren's **St Margaret Lothbury**, notable for its fine 17thC woodwork. Next door notice No. 7, Victorian architecture at its most imaginative. Opposite, at the financial heart of the City, is ⑧ the **Bank of England**. The street walls are all that remain of Sir John Soane's first 'Old Lady of Threadneedle Street', a masterpiece, which later gave way to Sir Herbert Baker's lifeless 1920s enlargement. ⑨ Since the 1986 'Big Bang' the **Stock Exchange** floor, once crazy with activity, has lain all but deserted. ⑩ The bankers' **City Club**, a refreshing and suitably clubby piece of Italianate by Philip Hardwick, 1833. ⑪ Turretted High Victorian **Mappin & Webb** (jewellers) has fallen prey to a controversial new development designed by James Stirling and described by Prince Charles as looking like a "1930's wireless". ⑫ Lutyens's superb 1920s **Midland Bank** has grand marbled halls. ⑬ **Mansion House**, the Lord Mayor's official residence. Its unwieldy façade is by George Dance the Elder, 1739-52. The interior is worth the tour, especially the Egyptian Hall. ⑭ Founded by Sir Thomas Gresham in 1566 for international commerce, the **Royal Exchange** is now home to LIFFE, the Financial Futures Exchange. The present building dates from 1841. Worth a visit for some old-fashioned dealing, frenzied hand signals and all, on the trading floor. Along Cornhill, site of Roman London's forum and basilica, two Wren churches, **St Michael** ⑮ and **St Peter** ⑯ back onto a medieval maze of tiny alleys which surround the quiet church garden. ⑰ The remains of the Roman **Temple of Mithras**. ⑱ **St Stephen Walbrook**, one of Wren's most rewarding churches. ⑲ Nicholas Hawksmoor's arresting **St Mary Woolnoth**, strikingly different from any of his other strangely spookey churches, but no less lovely. ⑳ **Lombard Street**, named for the Italian bankers who traded here in the Middle Ages. ㉑ **St Edmund the King**, Wren again, but not a show-piece.

▼99

Notting Hill Gate

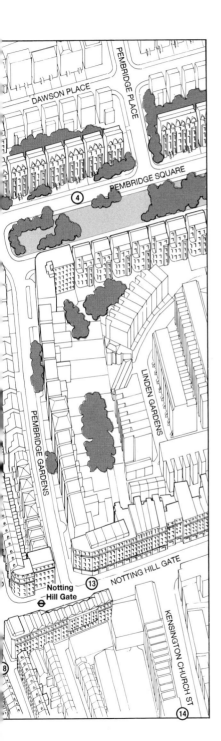

① **Chepstow Villas**, ② **Pembridge Crescent**, ③ **Pembridge Villas** and ④ **Pembridge Square** were all part of the Ladbroke Estate, owned and developed in the mid-19thC by James Weller Ladbroke, and leased to a Hereford man, W.K. Jenkins, who remembered his local towns in their names. Ladbroke planned the area as a 'garden city' and lined the streets with grand villas. His scheme included the Hippodrome racecourse, an unmitigated disaster, built by John Whyte around Ladbroke Grove. ⑤ London's most famous street market is held every Saturday in **Portobello Road**. It dates back to the 19thC, when gypsies traded horses here for the nearby racecourse. With the closure of the Caledonian Market in 1948, the antique dealers flocked in, and today the street is lined with stalls that sell everything from quality silver to bric-à-brac, second-hand records to fruit and veg. ⑥ **Kensington Park Road** was given its smart name in the 1840s, in the hope that it would lure the *beau monde* to an unfashionable address. ⑦ **Sun in Splendour**, friendly local, where in summer customers spill out on to the pavement. ⑧ New, inexpensive restaurant with a mixed menu, the **Gaffer** (££). ⑨ **John Oliver** (No. 33), interior designer who pioneered foil wallpaper in the 1960s. ⑩ Excellent selection of second-hand clothes for men at **John Burke & Partners** (No. 20). ⑪ **Savvas Kebab House** (No. 7), over 30 years old and still run by Savvas, an expansive Cypriot (£). ⑫ Above the Prince Albert pub, the fringe **Gate Theatre Club** excels in discovering new talent. ⑬ Until the 19thC, **Notting Hill Gate** was farmland. The gate was erected in the 18thC for the Uxbridge Turnpike Trust. A huge and colourful Caribbean Carnival is held every August Bank Holiday in the surrounding streets. ⑭ **Kensington Place**, buzzing, glamorous brasserie, where the food is really good value (££). **Gate Cinema** screens arty films. ⑯ Once the Gaumont Theatre, where Ellen Terry and Sarah Bernhardt strutted the boards, the **Coronet Cinema** still boasts W.G.R. Sprague's Italian Renaissance façade and its sumptuous Louis XVI-style interior. ⑰ **Uxbridge Street**, on the site of Kensington Gravel Pits. ⑱ **Geales** (2 Farmer Street) for up-market fish and chips (£). ⑲ The grand town houses of **Campden Hill Road** were built in the 1860s for the wealthy, who came here for the sake of their constitutions.

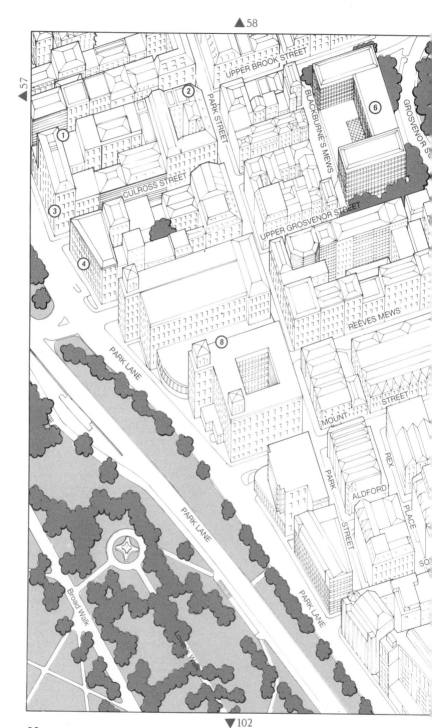

Grosvenor Square

Grosvenor Square Gardens

⑤

⑦

ADAM'S ROW

⑩

AUDLEY STREET

MOUNT STREET

GROSVENOR SQUARE

⑪

St George's Gardens

⑫   ⑬

SOUTH ST

SOUTH AUDLEY STREET

STREET

HILL STREET

DEANERY ST

▶82

① **Nos 33** (particularly fine), **35 and 36 Upper Brook Street** are good examples of original Grosvenor Estate houses (see below), most of which have been replaced or re-modelled. ② **Le Gavroche** (No. 43), a *grande dame* amongst London restaurants, run by the famous Roux brothers (**£££**). ③ **Dudley House** (No. 100), the only mansion (built in 1827) to have survived the ravaging of Park Lane. ④ **Nos 93-99**, set back from the dual carriageway, are also survivors. In the 19thC all Park Lane looked like this terrace, the fashionable houses embellished with Regency bows and cast-iron verandas. Disraeli lived at No. 93 1839-72. ⑤ **Grosvenor Square**, London's largest, lies at the heart of the great Grosvenor Estate, though today it is sadly devoid of original building or character (save the statues of Roosevelt and, recently, Eisenhower). The judicious Grosvenor family, headed by the Duke of Westminster, have profited enormously from this Mayfair estate (built 1720-75), and their equally prestigious Belgravia one (*see page 121*). Grosvenor streets continue to be as exclusive as ever. ⑥ Eero Saarinen's fussy **US Embassy** (1956-9) is notable for its sheer size rather than its irritating looks. ⑦ The **Britannia Hotel**, recently refurbished executive hotel. ⑧ **Grosvenor House Hotel** (built 1928), flagship of the Trust House Forte group, stands on the site of a celebrated Grosvenor family mansion. During World War II its famous Great Room was used as a mess for American officers, including Eisenhower and Patton; now a ballroom. ⑨ Still part of the Grosvenor Estate, **Mount Street** was entirely rebuilt in the late 19thC; its ornate terracotta-coloured houses recall the heyday of the British Empire. At ⑩ No. 14 is **Bonsack**, over-the-top baths for over-the-top people. From its inception Mayfair was studded with high-class shops. In ⑪ **South Audley Street** are: the **Counter Spy Shop** (No. 62), the place to go for bugging your worst enemy or foiling your would-be kidnapper; **James Purdey & Sons** (No. 57), all you need for slaughtering the furry and the feathered in style; **Hobbs** (No. 29), lavish food shop; and **Thomas Goode & Co** (No. 19), matchless glass and china shop established in 1845. The interior is sumptuous and two huge Minton elephants stand guard. *The* place for a wedding list. Close by ⑫ the colonial-style **Grosvenor Chapel** is curiously modest for the area. Behind it is ⑬ the delightful, oddly-shaped and secretive garden of St George's, **Hanover Square**.

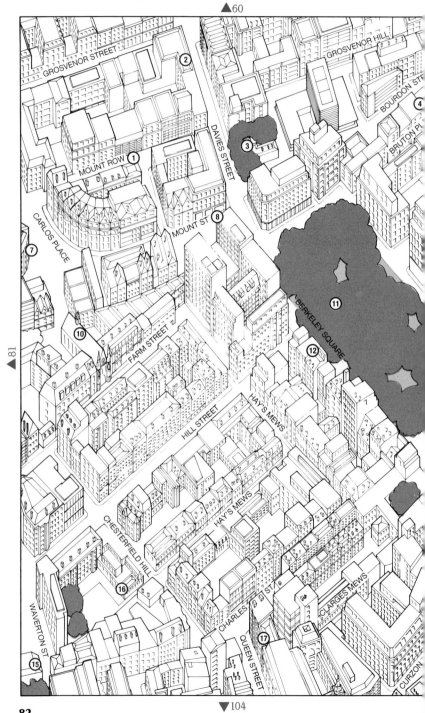

Berkeley Square

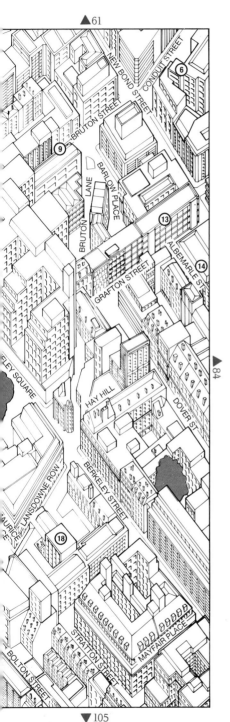

▲61

① **Mount Row**, unusual street of brick town houses, each different. ② **One Two Three** (No. 27), more formal sister to Ikeda (*see page 61*; **£££**). ③ **Bourdon House** (1723-5), showroom for Mallett's garden statuary. It looks every inch the private town house it once was. ④ **The Guinea** (No. 30), classy Mayfair pub-restaurant, dating from the 15thC (**£££**). Its well-known restaurant moved with the landlord to ⑤ **Grieg's Grill** (No. 26) when the lease reverted to the brewers in 1982 (**£££**). ⑥ The influence of its American namesake can still be felt in the décor and dry martinis of the **Westbury Hotel.** ⑦ **The Connaught,** hotel, restaurant and grill room: much vaunted, unfailingly excellent, but no fireworks (**£££**). ⑧ Poulterers John Baily & Sons now **Baily Lamartine** have been at No. 116 since 1790 when building of the Grosvenor Estate (*see page 81*), on which Mount Street stands, was first begun. At No. 20 is the venerable and violently expensive fish restaurant **Scott's** (No. 20). and **La Seppia** (No. 8a); (both **£££**). ⑨ Royal connections abound in **Bruton Street** with a plaque marking the Queen's birthplace at No. 17, the royal couturier **Hartnell** at No. 26, the Queen Mother's florist **Moyses Stevens** at No. 6 and the Duke of Edinburgh's gunmakers **Holland and Holland** at No. 33. ⑩ **Church of the Immaculate Conception**. Lavish 19thC Jesuit church with a Pugin altar. The favourite choice for smart Catholic weddings. Nearby are tranquil public gardens. ⑪ Stately 200-year-old plane trees and an elegant west side are the saving graces of **Berkeley Square**, otherwise dominated by offices and **Jack Barclay's** gleaming Rolls Royces. ⑫ *Pièce de résistance* is William Kent's No. 44, now the **Clermont** gambling club, preserved as the finest example of a London town house with a sensational interior. In its basement is **Annabel's**, the hermetically discreet, ever-fashionable private night club. ⑬ No. 14a, showcase of the imaginative designer **Zandra Rhodes**, especially noted since the 1970s for her evening wear. ⑭ **The Royal Institution**. At the turn of the 18thC chemistry professor Humphry Davy caused women to swoon during his lectures on account of his good looks. His successor Michael Faraday conducted his electricity experiments here in the 1830s (laboratory open twice weekly). ⑮ **Red Lion**, delightful old 'country' pub serving real ales and English food. ⑯ **The Greenhouse** (No. 27a), hidden mews restaurant with an international menu (**££**). ⑰ **Zen Central** (No. 10), Chinese *haute cuisine* in minimalist surroundings (**£££**). ⑱ **The May Fair**, de luxe hotel.

▶84

▼105

83

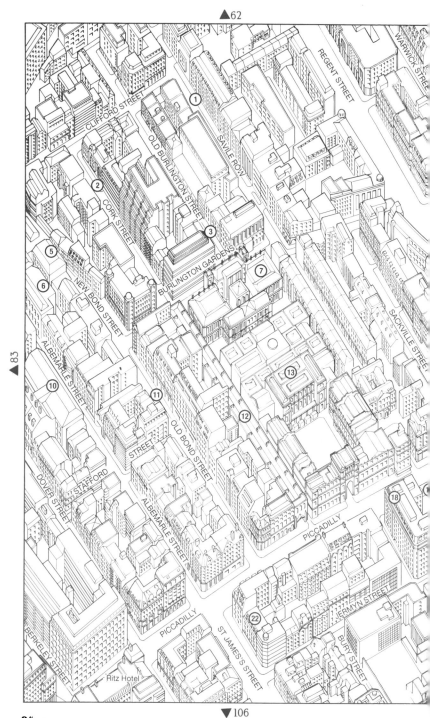

◀83

Piccadilly

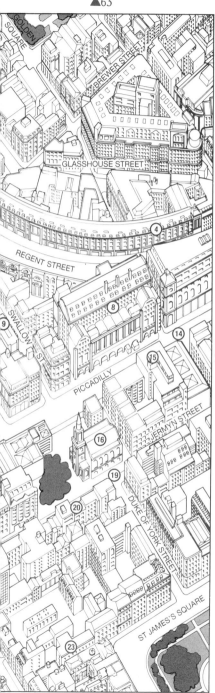

① Nowhere can match the quality, cut or price of a **Savile Row** suit. Famous names include **Gieves & Hawkes** (No. 1), **Hardy Amies** (No. 14) and trendier **Tommy Nutter** (No. 19). ② **Cork Street**, where prestigious art galleries abound. ③ **Old Burlington Street** (18thC), main route through the Burlington Estate. ④ **Café Royal**, with its opulent rococo Grill Room (**£££**) in the Quadrant (*see page 63*). ⑤ **Asprey** (Nos 165-169), the ultimate gift shop. ⑥ **Royal Institution**, its classical façade by Lewis Vulliamy. ⑦ **Museum of Mankind**, the British Museum's ethnography department. ⑧ Norman Shaw's Piccadilly Hotel, extravagantly refurbished and now known as the **Meridien**. Its sumptuous Edwardian **Oak Room Restaurant** boasts a Michelin star (**£££**). ⑨ **Bentley's**, authentic old oyster bar (**££**). ⑩ Civilized wood-panelled **Brown's Hotel**, the best place in London for afternoon tea. ⑪ Among **Old Bond Street**'s chic expensive shops are **Ferragamo** (No. 24), **Chanel** (No. 26), **Gucci** (No. 27) and **Charbonnel et Walker** (No. 28) for delectable chocolates. ⑫ Charming Regency **Burlington Arcade**, built by Samuel Ware for Lord Cavendish to prevent passers-by from throwing litter into his garden. Lined with exclusive shops selling every luxury, from cashmere sweaters to Irish linen, it is still patrolled by beadles. ⑬ **Royal Academy of Arts**, whose home, Burlington House is a fine example of Palladian architecture. Its excellent temporary exhibitions include the Summer Exhibition, a showcase for established and aspiring artists. ⑭ **Piccadilly**. The origin of the name lies with Robert Baker, a 17thC Strand tailor, who, with money he made from selling stiff collars called 'picadils', built a house, derisively known as 'Piccadilly Hall'. ⑮ **Simpson**, for men's and women's fashion. ⑯ **St James's**. Inside Wren's simple brick church there is a large galleried room with a decorated vaulted ceiling. ⑰ **Hatchard's**, for a huge selection of books. ⑱ **Fortnum & Mason**, luxury grocery store, where assistants in tails sell you anything from *foie gras* to *marrons glacés*. ⑲ Having been measured for his suits in Savile Row, the traditional English gentleman will go to **Jermyn Street** for his shirts. ⑳ At **Paxton & Whitfield**, choose from over 300 different cheeses. ㉑ 1960s **Cavendish Hotel**, on the site of the old hotel, run by Edward VII's friend Rosa Lewis, 'the Duchess of Jermyn Street'. ㉒ **White's**, St James's oldest, smartest gentleman's club. ㉓ **London Library**, founded by Carlyle. ㉔ **Quaglino's**, London's most talked about restaurant, is set in a famous old '30s favourite (**£££**).

86 ►

▲64

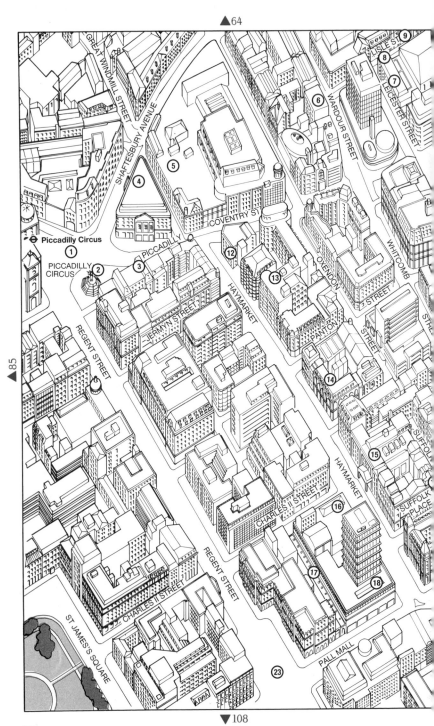

Piccadilly Circus

▼108

Piccadilly Circus/Leicester Square

① That perennially favourite meeting-place, **Piccadilly Circus**, lacks all the grandeur that John Nash envisaged for it, though its tawdry image has been smartened up of late. ② London's most famous statue is not in fact of **Eros**, God of Love, but the Angel of Christian Charity, a memorial to philanthropist Lord Shaftesbury. ③ The lovely **Criterion Brasserie** (£) and **Theatre**, by Thomas Verity (1870-4). ④ The **London Pavilion** and ⑤ the **Trocadero** were once variety theatres, now restored as shopping and entertainment complexes; the **Guinness World of Records** exhibition in the Trocadero is worth visiting. Back in Chinatown (*see page 65*) ⑥ **Chuen Cheng Ku** (No. 17) is a vast emporium for *dim sum* (££), while ⑦ **Poons** (No. 4) is known for its wind-dried foods (££). ⑧ **Manzi's** (No. 1) is an Italian survivor – family run, with an almost pre-war ambience (bustling downstairs, calmer upstairs), and good simple fish dishes (££). ⑨ In Chinese **Lisle Street** try perhaps **Fung Shing** (No. 15; ££) or the **New Diamond** (No. 23; ££). ⑩ Visit the church of **Notre Dame de France** to see frescoes by Jean Cocteau. ⑪ Difficult to believe that characterless, commercialized **Leicester Square** was one of London's first (1670s) and grandest squares. In Victorian times it became *the* centre of entertainment; with the arrival of the movies its famous theatres became cinemas. ⑫ Notice **Paperchase's** rare 18thC shop-front (No. 34). ⑬ The **Design Centre** (No. 28): the best of British design. Behind, at 1 Oxendon Street, is the excellent **Crafts Council Gallery**. ⑭ **Burberry's** (Nos 18-22), the last word in rainwear since 1856. Two fine theatres are ⑮ Nash's **Theatre Royal, Haymarket** (which was once just that) and ⑯ **Her Majesty's**, rebuilt in 1897 by C.J. Phipps. ⑰ The perfect **Royal Opera Arcade** (Nash and Repton, 1816). ⑱ **New Zealand House**, ugly and obtrusive. ⑲ Had Nash's grand plan (*see page 109*) been carried out to the full, all the surrounding side-streets would have looked like **Suffolk Street** and **Place**. ⑳ Sir Robert Smirke's **Canada House** (1824-7, later messily extended). ㉑ William Wilkins's ineffectual **National Gallery** (1832-8) houses quite simply the cream of European painting; easy to get round with magnificent interiors by E.M. Barry and the benefit of the new Sainsbury wing. ㉒ The **National Portrait Gallery**. A fascinating record of what the great names in English history and the arts really looked like. ㉓ The **Crimean War Memorial** (1862) depicts Florence Nightingale and her lamp.

▶88

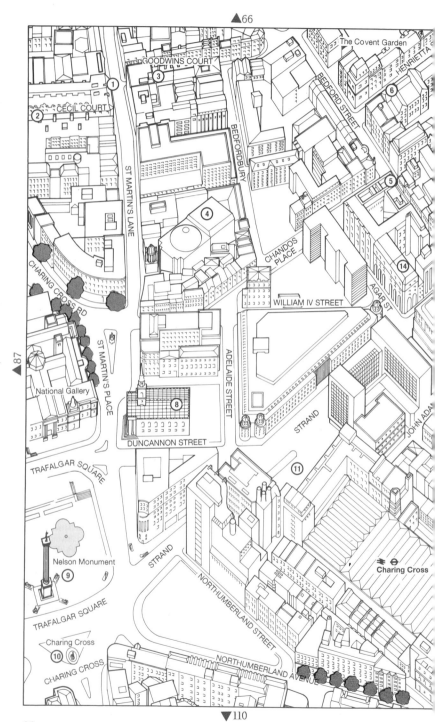

▲66

The Covent Garden

GOODWINS COURT

HENRIETTA

BEDFORD STREET

①

CECIL COURT

②

③

⑥

BEDFORDBURY

⑤

④

CHANDOS PLACE

ST MARTIN'S LANE

⑭

CHARING CROSS RD

WILLIAM IV STREET

AGAR ST

▲87

ST MARTIN'S PLACE

ADELAIDE STREET

National Gallery

⑧

STRAND

JOHN ADAM

DUNCANNON STREET

⑪

TRAFALGAR SQUARE

Nelson Monument

STRAND

⑨

≠ ⊖
Charing Cross

TRAFALGAR SQUARE

NORTHUMBERLAND STREET

Charing Cross

⑩

CHARING CROSS

NORTHUMBERLAND AVENUE

▼110

Trafalgar Square/Strand

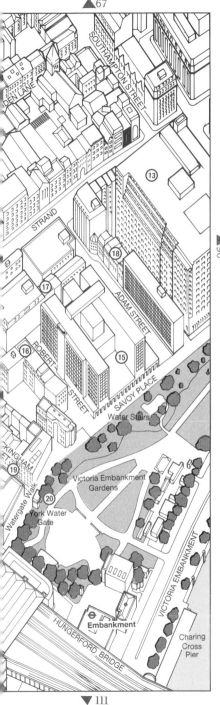

▲67

⑬

⑱

⑰

⑯ ⑮

⑲

⑳

90 ▶

111 ▼

Water Stairs

Victoria Embankment
Gardens

York Water
Gate

Embankment

Charing
Cross
Pier

① The **Salisbury** has a sumptuous Victorian interior. ② **Cecil Court** is a pedestrian haven for second-hand book browsers. ③ **Goodwins Court**, a little slice of the 18thC. The fire-mark (look hard) above the arch shows the buildings were insured and would be saved by the insurers' fire-fighters. ④ The **Coliseum** was built as an Edwardian palace of variety and is now home to the English National Opera. ⑤ If you are with children, head for **TGI Fridays** (6 Bedford Street) for lunch (**££**). ⑥ **Henrietta Street**, named in honour of Queen Henrietta Maria, wife of Charles I. ⑦ **Rules** (35 Maiden Lane) has fortified English stomachs since 1798 (**£££**). ⑧ **St Martin-in-the-Fields**, apart from its beauty (James Gibbs, 1722), is one of London's liveliest churches (lunchtime concerts, crafts, brass rubbing centre, excellent restaurant, **Café in the Crypt £**. ⑨ **Trafalgar Square** was first cleared as part of a grand improvement scheme by John Nash, but was designed after his death by Sir Charles Barry (1840). Towering above the pigeons is one-eyed, one-armed Nelson (1843), guarded by Landseer's lions (1867). The fountains were added by Lutyens in 1939. Around the perimeter of the square, much redevelopment is in progress. ⑩ A **statue of Charles I**, dating from his reign, stands on the site of the original Charing Cross. This marked the last resting place of the body of Edward I's wife, Queen Eleanor, on the journey from Nottingham to her burial at Westminster Abbey in 1290. ⑪ A Victorian replica of the **Charing Cross** stands outside the station of the same name. ⑫ The **Strand**, originally a riverside bridle-way, was once lined with Tudor palaces. ⑬ **Shell-Mex House** began life in 1885 as the Cecil Hotel, then the largest in Europe. ⑭ The statues on **Zimbabwe House** by Jacob Epstein caused a furore when they were unveiled in 1908. In 1930 they were mutilated in the name of decency and safety after a male member had fallen off and hit an innocent passer-by. ⑮ The 20thC **Adelphi** stands on the site of an architectural masterpiece by the Adam brothers (1770s), which was a speculative riverside development. Its central terrace of houses was sadly destroyed in 1932. Survivors can be seen at ⑯ **1-3 Robert Street**, ⑰ **8 John Adam Street** (Royal Society of Arts) and ⑱ **7 Adam Street**. ⑲ Attractive **Buckingham Street** was home to Samuel Pepys, first at No. 12 and then No. 14. ⑳ The imposing riverside entrance to York House, **York Water Gate** (now land-locked) is the only reminder of the Strand's palaces.

▲68

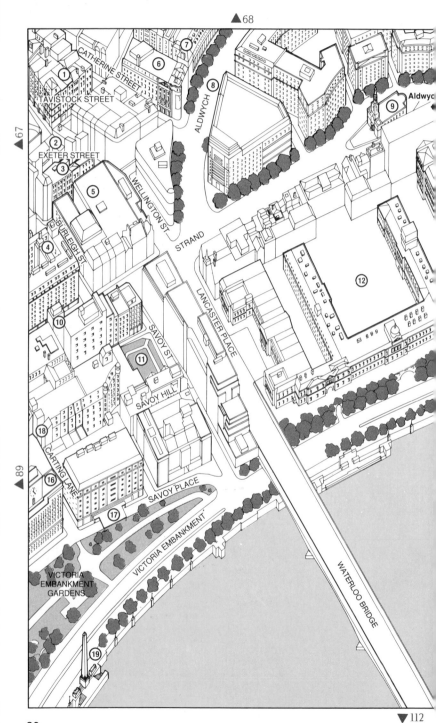

▲67

▲89

CATHERINE STREET

TAVISTOCK STREET

EXETER STREET

BURLEIGH ST

WELLINGTON ST

ALDWYCH

STRAND

Aldwych

LANCASTER PLACE

SAVOY ST

SAVOY HILL

SAVOY PLACE

CARTING LANE

VICTORIA EMBANKMENT

VICTORIA EMBANKMENT GARDENS

WATERLOO BRIDGE

▼112

Strand/Aldwych

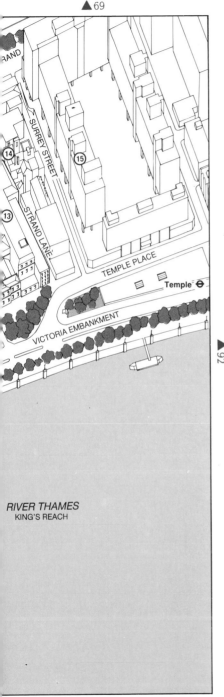

▲69

SURREY STREET

⑭

⑮

⑬

STRAND LANE

TEMPLE PLACE

Temple ⊖

VICTORIA EMBANKMENT

92

RIVER THAMES
KING'S REACH

▼113

① **Luigi's** (No. 15) has average Italian food, lots of pzazz, and walls crammed with photos of its board-treading patrons. ② Also theatrical, indeed positively star-studded, **Orso** (No. 27) sports a stylish Mediterranean interior, and some of the best modern Italian food in town (**£££**). Around the corner its older brother ③ **Joe Allen's** (No. 13) provides *bonhomie*, American food and more well-known faces to spot. ④ **The Strand Palace Hotel** is huge and excellent value, though there is no room service. ⑤ **The Lyceum** was the scene of actor Henry Irving's greatest triumphs. ⑥ W.G.R. Sprague's twin theatres, the **Strand** and **Aldwych** (*see page 69*) flank ⑦ the **Waldorf Hotel**, whose Palm Court teas and tea dances are still a perfect afternoon treat. ⑧ The crescent-shaped **Aldwych** (*see page 69*) links the Strand (*see page 89*) to Kingsway. ⑨ James Gibbs's delectable little baroque church, **St Mary-le-Strand** (1717). Battered by pelting traffic and a wartime bomb, it hangs grimly on, with the help of extensive restoration. ⑩ **Simpson's-in-the-Strand** (No. 100); unchanging bastion of upper-crust Britishness beloved for its excellent roast beef and soggy veg (**£££**). ⑪ **The Savoy Chapel**, intimate setting for society weddings, was rebuilt in 1820 by Robert Smirke, but dates back to the Tudor Savoy Palace. ⑫ Sir William Chambers' boldly classical but dull **Somerset House** (1776). The fine rooms above the *cour d'honneur* now house the **Courtauld Institute's Galleries**: six superb private art collections (open daily). ⑬ **King's College**, 1829, part of London University. ⑭ This **'Roman' bath** (No. 5: National Trust, view by appt.) certainly provided very cold plunges for Victorians, but probably not for Romans. ⑮ **Howard Hotel**, extravagant luxury for city-bound executives. ⑯ **Shell-Mex House**, 1931. ⑰ Ever-glamorous, with marvellous art deco accoutrements, the **Savoy Hotel** was built in 1881, next to ⑱ the **Savoy Theatre**, both financed by Richard d'Oyly Carte, the latter for his Gilbert and Sullivan productions. The theatre was gutted by fire, but has recently been lavishly restored to its former glory. ⑲ **Cleopatra's Needle**, ancient Egyptian obelisk presented to the British in 1819, and finally erected here in 1878. Beneath it was buried a Victorian 'time box', which contained such frivolous items as photographs of pretty ladies, hairpins, cigars and a railway guide.

LITTLE ESSEX STREET DEVEREUX COURT ▲70

① ② ③

④ ⑤ ⑥ ⑦

ESSEX STREET CROWN OFFICE ROW

KING'S WALK

⑪ ⑬ ⑭

⑰ ⑮

⑫ MIDDLE
TEMPLE LANE

⑯

TEMPLE PLACE

Victoria Embankment
Gardens Middle Temple Garden Inner Temple Garden

⑲ VICTORIA EMBANKMENT

⑳

Temple
Stairs
㉒

㉑

RIVER THAMES
KING'S REACH

◀91

Middle and Inner Temples

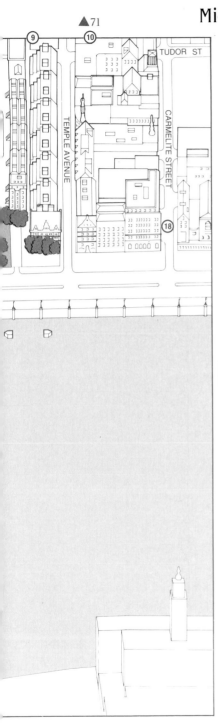

① **Cheshire Cheese** (5 Little Essex Street), friendly Jacobean pub with beams and an indigenous ghost. ② **Edgar Wallace** (40 Essex Street), a pub on the site of the Essex Head, where Dr Johnson founded the Essex Head Club in 1783. Rebuilt in the 19thC and decorated with Wallace memorabilia. ③ **Devereux Court**, named after Robert Devereux, Earl of Essex, whose mansion, Essex House, stood on the site. ④ **Essex Street**. 17thC speculative builder, Nicholas Barbon, demolished most of Essex Street to build a street of 'taverns, alehouses, cookshops and vaulting schools'. ⑤ **Middle Temple Hall** (1570) boasts a superb double hammerbeam roof and screen, both of oak, and a small table, 'the cupboard', reputedly made from wood of the *Golden Hind*. Readers' coats of arms decorate the walls. ⑥ **Lamb Buildings**, named after Charles Lamb, born in ⑦ **Crown Office Row**, where clerks of the Crown drew up indictments. ⑧ Wren's attractive **King's Bench Walk**. ⑨ The Walls of the aptly named **Witness Box** pub (36 Tudor Street) are papered with cuttings of crime stories. ⑩ **White Swan** (Nos 28-30), local pub for barristers and remaining Fleet Street reporters. ⑪ **Plowden Buildings** (1831) commemorate Edmund Plowden, Treasurer of Middle Temple and builder of the Hall. ⑫ **Middle** and ⑬ **Inner Temples**, named after the Knights Templar, who protected pilgrims in the Holy Land. The Order moved here from Holborn in the 12thC, grew wealthy, was persecuted and suppressed in the early 14thC. From 1608 law students leased its buildings. Barristers have remained here ever since, organized into two of the four Inns of Court. ⑭ **Wrought-iron gates**, decorated with the Gray's Inn griffin and Inner Temple pegasus to symbolize their friendship, stand at the entrace to ⑮ **Inner Temple Garden**, once scene of the Royal Horticultural Society Flower Show. ⑯ **Middle Temple Garden**, where the rival Dukes of Lancaster and York allegedly picked the red and white roses that became emblems of the Wars of the Roses. ⑰ **Middle Temple Library** (1956), by Sir Edward Maufe. ⑱ **Carmelite Street**, so-called because Edward I granted the land to the Carmelites, whose immunity from arrest turned the area into a thieves' hideout. ⑲ and ⑳ **Silver griffins** with red-veined wings mark the City boundary. ㉑ **HQS Wellington**, the Master Mariners' Livery Hall. ㉒ **Temple Stairs**, from where, traditionally, the Swan Uppers leave for Sunbury every July to mark the beaks of cygnets.

▲72

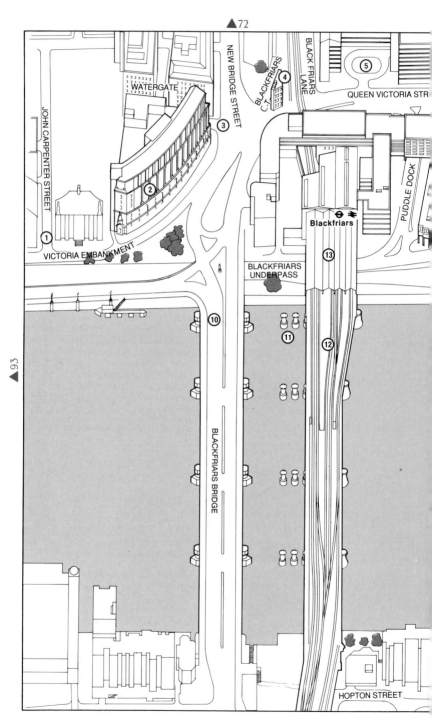

JOHN CARPENTER STREET

WATERGATE

NEW BRIDGE STREET

BLACK FRIARS LANE

BLACKFRIARS C.T.

④

⑤

QUEEN VICTORIA STR

③

②

PUDDLE DOCK

①

Blackfriars

⑬

VICTORIA EMBANKMENT

BLACKFRIARS UNDERPASS

▲93

⑩

⑪

⑫

BLACKFRIARS BRIDGE

HOPTON STREET

Blackfriars

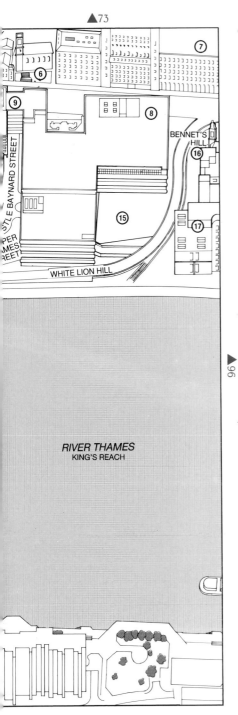

BENNET'S HILL

BAYNARD STREET

WHITE LION HILL

RIVER THAMES
KING'S REACH

① **John Carpenter Street** commemorates the Town Clerk of London, whose bequest in 1442 began the City of London School for Boys (see 17). ② **Unilever House**, a conspicuous 1930s building ornamented with statues. Near here stood the house of Dr Budd, where 14-year-old Emma Lyon, later Lady Hamilton, was housemaid. ③ Until Victorian times, the Thames was London's busiest thoroughfare. This street, **Watergate**, marks the old foreshore (before the Embankment was created), and one of the many watergates (this was for Bridewell Palace, *page 73*) where barges could be boarded and alighted. ④ The **Blackfriar**, an amazing wedge-shaped pub in the Arts and Crafts style. Its marble and bronze saloon bar has bronze friezes of monks; the 'side-chapel' bar is even more ornate, with an arched mosaic ceiling. ⑤ **Printing House Square**, site of *The Times* newspaper premises from its inception in 1788, until it moved in 1974. The huge sundial is by Henry Moore. ⑥ The last, plainest and cheapest of Wren's City churches, **St Andrew-by-the-Wardrobe** was built in 1685. Its name derives from the nearby King's Wardrobe where Edward I's ceremonial robes were kept. ⑦ **Faraday Building** (1933) is an early example of the many obtrusive buildings which have crept into the City's skyline in the 20thC. **Baynard House**, ⑧ is another. At one corner, No. 135 is ⑨ the **Telecom Technology Showcase** (open Mon-Fri). ⑩ **Blackfriars Bridge**: built 1760, replaced 1860; widened 1910. The River Fleet, from Hampstead, once flowed into the Thames here; now it is covered by Farringdon Street. The **western railway bridge** ⑪ (impressive cast-iron columns) was built at the same time as the road bridge (both Joseph Cubitt); the eastern one ⑫ some 20 years later. ⑬ **Blackfriars Station**, one of a string built by the Victorians (1864), but now superceded by the adjoining underground station. Blackfriars takes its name from a prosperous Dominican monastery, which stood on this land until the Dissolution in 1538. ⑭ Sir Bernard Miles's **Mermaid Theatre**, launched in 1959 (bar and restaurant). ⑮ The **site of Baynard's Castle**, first built by a companion of William the Conqueror. Subsequently rebuilt three times, it became a royal residence, and was finally destroyed in the Great Fire in 1666. ⑯ **St Benet**, a Wren gem, c1680, with garlanded windows, a charming tower and simple, affecting interior. Since 1879 a Welsh church. ⑰ The new (1986) **City of London School**.

96

Southwark Bridge

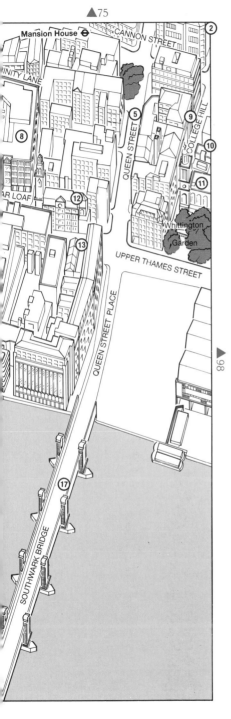

(1) **Distaff Lane**, where the distaffs used for spinning were made and sold. (2) Wine merchants from Le Riole in Bordeaux gave **Tower Royal** its name. Edward III owned a mansion here, which contained Queen Philippa's Wardrobe. Neglected by the 16thC, it was used to stable royal horses. (3) Responsible for recording Arms and pedigrees, the **College of Arms** is housed in a 17thC mellow brick building with splendid wrought-iron gates from Goodrich Court. (4) After the Fire, 12thC **St Nicholas Cole Abbey** was rebuilt by Wren in classical style. Although devastated in 1941, it retains some original 17thC woodwork. (5) **Queen Street** follows the route of the long-vanished Soper Lane, where the soapmakers lived and worked. (6) Imposing 1960s **Salvation Army International HQ**. (7) **Huggin Hill** takes its name from the Anglo-Saxon word 'hoggene', 'where hogs are kept'. (8) **Beaver House** was the London HQ of the Hudson's Bay Company, which traded in furs and skins from the American Indians. Fur auctions are still held here, and the smell of the chemical used to preserve them pervades the surrounding area. (9) Dick Whittington owned a house in **College Hill**, named after the College of St Spirit and St Mary, which he founded. (10) **Whittington's** (No. 21), wine bar in the legendary man's own vaulted cellars. (11) Wren's **St Michael Paternoster Royal**, bombed in 1944 and rebuilt in 1967, where Dick Whittington is buried – a window depicts him with his cat. (12) **St James Garlickhithe**, a Wren church with a distinctive steeple of three stone temples. A mummified body is kept in a cupboard in the vestry. (13) The late 17thC **Vintners' Hall** has an anonymous painted sculpture, *Vintry Schoolboy*, on the west wall. (14) **Stew Lane**, where whores allegedly boarded boats to cross the river to the stews, or brothels, of Bankside. (15) **Queenhithe**, where Queen Matilda built the city's first public lavatory in the early 12thC. In the Middle Ages it was London's most important dock, but declined in the 15thC. (16) **Samuel Pepys**, pub in a converted warehouse with good views of the river. The restaurant serves hearty English food (£). (17) **Southwark Bridge**, rebuilt by Sir Ernest George in 1912-21. (18) **Emerson Street**, location of the replica Globe Theatre, due to open in 1992. (19) On the site of a bear-baiting arena, Bear Gardens is home to the **Shakespeare Globe Museum**.

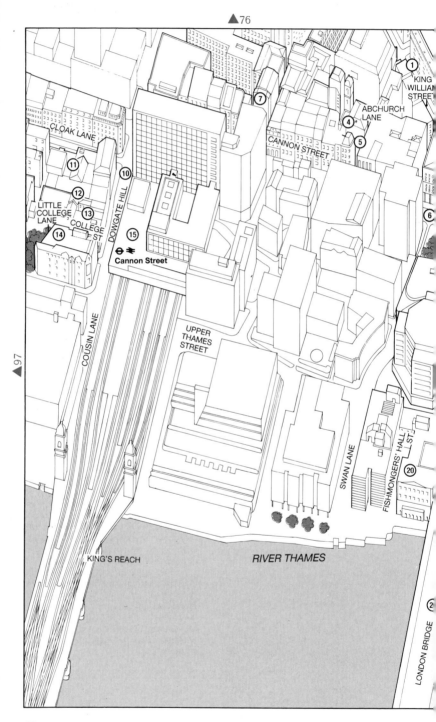

▲76

KING
WILLIAM
STREET

ABCHURCH
LANE

CLOAK LANE

CANNON STREET

LITTLE
COLLEGE
LANE

COLLEGE
ST

DOWGATE HILL

Cannon Street

COUSIN LANE

UPPER
THAMES
STREET

SWAN LANE

FISHMONGERS' HALL
ST

KING'S REACH

RIVER THAMES

LONDON BRIDGE

Cannon Street

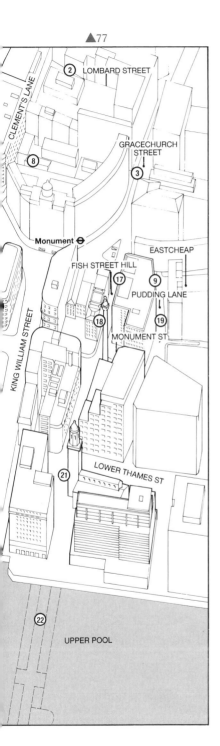

① **King William Street** (1829-35) commemorates William IV. **②** **Lombard Street**. 12thC Italian financiers gave London's prime banking street its name. Attractive medieval signs still hang outside the banks. **③** **Gracechurch Street**, named after St Benet's Grass, a Wren church, later demolished. **④** In a pretty cobbled yard, Wren's **Guild Church of St Mary Abchurch** (1686) has a red-brick Dutch-style exterior and splendid interior, with painted dome by William Snow and genuine Grinling Gibbons reredos. **⑤** **Abchurch Lane**, best known in the 17thC for Mother Wells' bakery and the French eating-house, Pontack's, favoured by the literati. **⑥** **Cannon Street**. The name derives from Candlewick, a reference to the candlemakers who lived here in the Middle Ages. **⑦** **The London Stone** is embedded in the wall of No. 111, on the site of St Swithin's, a Wren Church destroyed in the Second World War. **⑧** **St Clement's Eastcheap**, also by Wren. **⑨** **Eastcheap**, famous for its medieval meat market. **⑩** **Dowgate Hill**, home to several City Livery Companies: **⑪** **Tallow Chandlers' Hall** (No. 4), **⑫** **Skinners' Hall** (No. 8), **⑬** **Dyers' Hall** (No. 10) and **⑭** **Innholders' Hall** (29 College Street). **⑮** Hawkshaw's **Cannon Street Station** (1866), rebuilt in the 1960s. **⑯** **Square Rigger** (32 King William Street), nautical pub. **⑰** **Fish Street Hill**, where fishmongers were permitted to trade. **⑱** **The Monument** (1677), built by Wren to commemorate the Great Fire of 1666. Topped by a gilded urn, the 202ft Doric column is the same height as its distance from the site of the baker's shop in **⑲** **Pudding Lane** where the fire started. **⑳** **Fishmongers' Hall**, magnificent Greek Revival building by Henry Roberts and Sir George Gilbert Scott. Its treasures include the dagger used to kill Wat Tyler, a 16thC funeral pall and a fine collection of paintings. **㉑** On the site of an 11thC church, Wren's **St Magnus**. Through its arch was the entrance to **㉒** **Old London Bridge** (1176). On the site of a wooden Roman bridge, it was made of stone, built up with houses and fortified with iron spikes, where heads of traitors were displayed. **㉓** A new **London Bridge** was built upstream in 1831, but was subsequently sold and transported to an Arizona amusement park in 1971. The present bridge, with three concrete arches, dates from 1973.

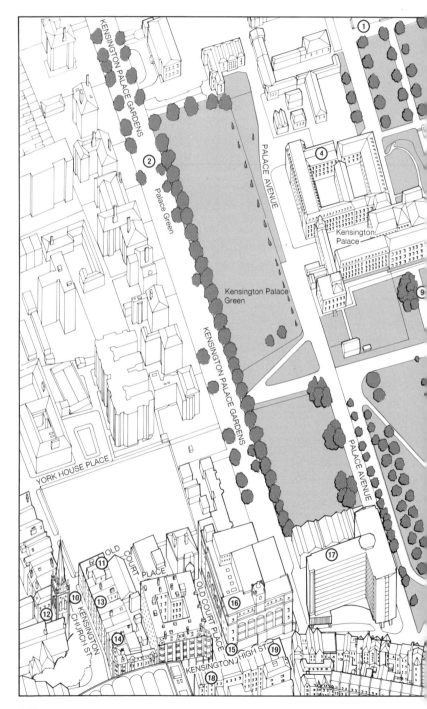

Kensington Gardens

① Queen Anne held tea parties in her **Orangery** (1704-5), attributed to Hawksmoor. ② **Kensington Palace Gardens** and **Palace Green**, private avenue built on the palace kitchen garden in the 19thC by Sir James Pennethorne. Its sumptuous mansions, now mostly embassies, earned the road the title 'Millionaires' Row'. ③ Delightful Edwardian **sunken garden** with flower beds and pond enclosed by pleached limes. ④ "The house is very noble, tho not great . . . the Gardens about it very delicious", 17thC diarist John Evelyn's description of **Kensington Palace**. A Jacobean house that became a royal palace when William III bought it from the Earl of Nottingham in 1689, and instructed Wren to improve it. He enlisted the help of Hawksmoor, William Kent and Grinling Gibbons. Members of the royal family still have apartments here, and the State Apartments are open to the public. ⑤ Handsome Carrara marble **statue of Queen Victoria** by her daughter Princess Louise (1893). ⑥ When George II opened the 275-acre **Kensington Gardens** to 'respectably dressed people' on Saturdays, the ⑦ **Broad Walk** became one of the most fashionable places in which to promenade. ⑧ **Round Pond**, where children sail toy boats and fish for sticklebacks. ⑨ **Bronze of William III** by Heinrich Baucke (1907). ⑩ **Kensington Church Street**, once a country lane with a toll gate, now known for its pricey boutiques and antique shops. ⑪ **Maggie Jones's** (6 Old Court Place), honest English food served in country kitchen-style restaurant. ⑫ **St Mary Abbots**, founded by the Abbot of Abingdon in the 12thC, but later rebuilt, most recently in Early English style by Sir George Gilbert Scott. It has an unusual vaulted cloister. ⑬ **Jimmie's Wine Bar** (No. 18), haunt of the Kensington set. ⑭ **Crabtree and Evelyn** (No. 6), bursting with beautifully packaged, delicious-smelling lotions and potions. ⑮ **Kensington High Street**, one of London's major shopping streets. ⑯ **Hyper Hyper** (Nos 26-40), for trendy off-beat clothes. ⑰ Richard Seifert's **Royal Garden Hotel** (1965) boasts a panoramic view from its roof-top restaurant. ⑱ **Kensington Market** (Nos 49-53) had its heyday in the early 1970s, and still sells Indian cotton clothes and junk jewellery. ⑲ **Andronicas Coffee Shop** (No. 35), excellent for coffee and Danish pastries.

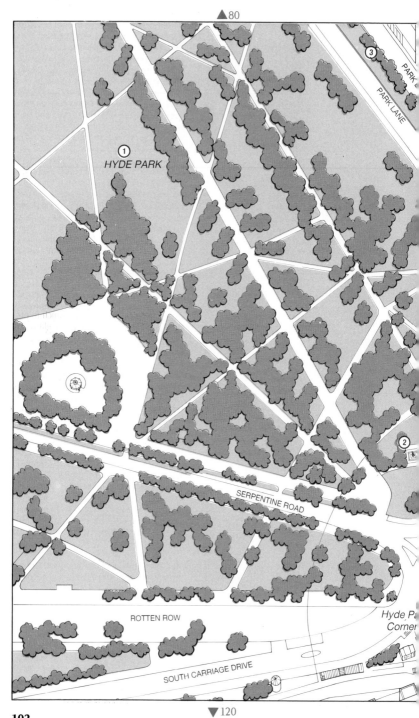

HYDE PARK

PARK

PARK LANE

SERPENTINE ROAD

Hyde Park
Corner

ROTTEN ROW

SOUTH CARRIAGE DRIVE

Park Lane

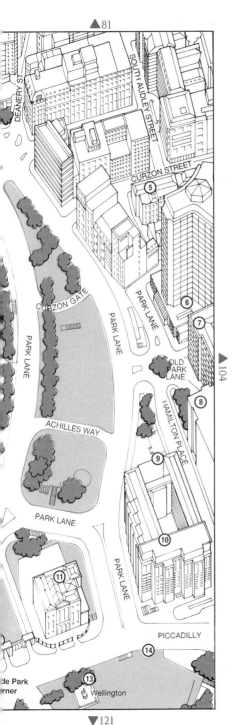

① **Hyde Park** combines with Kensington Gardens to form the city's largest open space – an immense 618 acres – which keeps Londoners breathing freely. A royal park since Henry VIII appropriated it (Cromwell sold it off; Charles II took it back), Hyde Park has seen countless pageants, parades, spectacles, duels, firework displays, even the odd pop concert. Its feeling of informality is enhanced by the Serpentine (added 1730s; off map) for boating or swimming (even on Christmas Day for the truly hardy). Don't miss the lovely view from John Rennie's 1826 bridge. ② **Achilles**, Britain's first public nude statue (1882) was a grave embarrassment to the 'women of England', who had commissioned it to honour the Duke of Wellington. ③ **Park Lane** was once just that – a muddy parkside lane. After the improvements to Hyde Park Corner (*see page 121*), it became, from the 1820s, London's most fashionable street. Today it is a dual carriageway lined by well-known hotels. ④ Dorchester House, a 'private palace' built by Lewis Vulliamy for a mid-19thC millionaire, made way in 1931 for the **Dorchester Hotel**. A London landmark, it looks in stunning shape these days. ⑤ Disraeli died at **No. 19** in 1881. ⑥ Marvellous view from the Roof Restaurant and bar of the **Hilton**, particularly as, for once, the 28-storey hotel is not in it. ⑦ The **Londonderry Hotel**. ⑧ The **Inn on the Park**, glamorous, superbly run hotel favoured by stars. ⑨ **Nos 4 and 5** (Les Ambassadeurs Club) are surviving aristocrats' houses now trapped between the Inn on the Park and ⑩ the **Inter-Continental Hotel**. ⑪ Once the first in a row of fine mansions, **Apsley House** (also known as No. 1 London) stands isolated and almost impenetrable, cut off by the traffic thundering past on three sides. Built by Adam (1771-8), it was later aggrandised by the victorious Duke of Wellington and his architect, Benjamin Wyatt. Now the **Wellington Museum**, it is filled with the Duke's fabulous spoils of war, including an astonishing statue by Canova of Napoleon, put thoroughly in his place. Adam's genius is shown off in the lovely Piccadilly Drawing Room, and Wyatt's in the glittering Waterloo Gallery. (Closed Mon.) ⑫ Decimus Burton's **screen**, designed as a park entrance in 1825, is most elegant but now looks sadly out of place. ⑬ **Equestrian statue of Wellington** astride his heroic horse, Copenhagen (buried with full military honours), by Sir Joseph Edgar Boehm (1888). ⑭ **Statue of David**, a memorial to the Machine Gun Corps, by Francis Derwent Wood (1925).

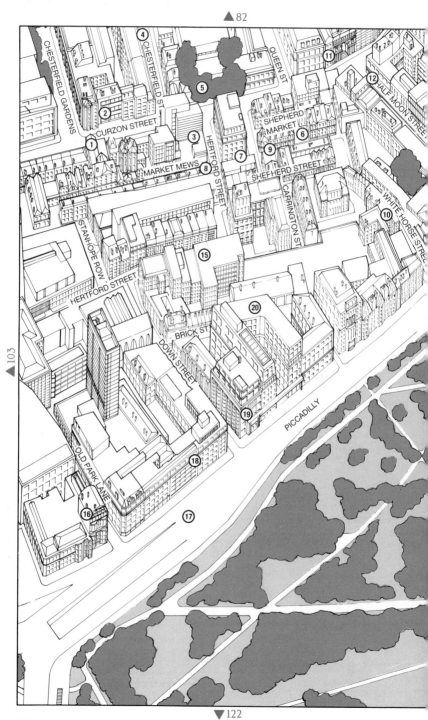

CHESTERFIELD GARDENS

CHESTERFIELD ST

QUEEN ST

HALF MOON STREET

CURZON STREET

SHEPHERD MARKET

MARKET MEWS

HERTFORD STREET

SHEPHERD STREET

WHITE HORSE STREET

STANHOPE ROW

CARRINGTON ST

HERTFORD STREET

BRICK ST

DOWN STREET

OLD PARK LANE

PICCADILLY

Shepherd Market/Green Park

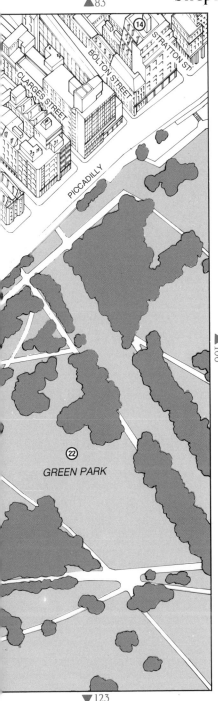

▲83

106 ▶

⑭

BOLTON STREET

CLARGES STREET

STRATTON ST.

PICCADILLY

㉒

GREEN PARK

▼123

① **Curzon Street** sports a number of exclusive gambling clubs amongst its terraced houses, notably **Crockfords** which occupies the magnificent Adam ballroom at No. 30. ② **Brinkley's Champagne Bar** (No. 17c) serves Mayfair's favourite tipple (**££**). ③ The **Curzon Cinema** has wonderfully comfy seats, but the excellent foreign films should keep you awake. ④ **Chesterfield Street**, Mayfair's best preserved 18thC street; little has changed since Beau Brummel lived at No. 4. ⑤ **Crewe House** (c1730, façade 1813), a rare surviving example of Mayfair's grand houses set in their own grounds. It was built by architect Edward Shepherd who laid out ⑥ **Shepherd Market**. A maze of narrow lanes brimming with pretty houses, shops, cafés and pubs, it still retains a strong flavour of its notorious past when it was the site of the bawdy May Fairs. Noteworthy restaurants here include: ⑦ **Tiddy Dols** (55 Shepherd Market) with traditional English food and 'Elizabethan' entertainment aimed more at the tourist than the gourmet (**££**); two excellent Lebanese restaurants, ⑧ **Al Sultan** (51-52 Hertford Street; **££**) and ⑨ **Al Hamra** (31-32 Shepherd Market; **££**); and ⑩ for top Malaysian food, tropically decorated **Straits** (5 Whitehorse Street; **££**). ⑪ **George F. Trumper** (No. 9), gentlemen's hairdresser and perfumer since 1875. ⑫ Many well-known people have resided in Half Moon Street, including Boswell, Hazlitt and Shelley, but none more so than the fictional creations of P.G. Woodhouse – Bertie Wooster and his man Jeeves. ⑬ **Miyama** (No. 38), refined Japanese restaurant with high standards of cooking (**£££**). ⑭ **Langan's** (No. 26). London's most exciting dining room is still buzzing, though there are as many star spotters as stars these days (**£££**). ⑮ Playwright and MP Richard Sheridan lived at No. 10 (designed by Robert Adam), as did General Burgoyne. ⑯ Queue up for the best hamburgers in town at the **Hard Rock Café** (No. 150; **££**). ⑰ The great private houses of **Piccadilly** have given way to clubs and hotels. ⑱ **Cavalry and Guards Club** (No. 127), bastion of bowler and brolly. ⑲ Luxurious extra touches, especially appreciated by women guests, distinguish the **Athenaeum Hotel**. The **Park Lane Hotel** next door, ⑳ is still privately owned, unstinting on art deco style and space. ㉑ **Naval and Military Club**, affectionately known as the 'In and Out', after the words on the gateposts. ㉒ **Green Park** – limes, poplars, plane trees and deck-chairs.

▲84

Green Park ⊖

PICCADILLY

ARLINGTON ST

PARK PLACE

ST JAMES'S STREET

BURY STREET

RYDER ST.

ST JAMES'S PLACE

ST JAMES'S PLACE

QUEEN'S WALK

QUEEN'S WALK

CATHERINE WHEEL YARD

LITTLE ST JAMES'S STREET

CLEVELAND ROW

STABLE YARD

STABLE YARD

GREEN PARK

①
②
③
④
⑤
⑥
⑨
⑩
⑪
⑫
⑭
⑲
⑳

St James's Palace

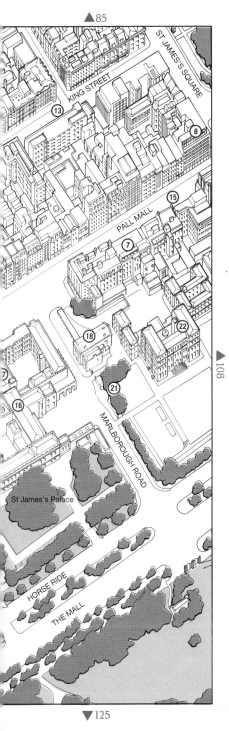

St James's Palace

THE MALL

① **The Ritz**. Lunch overlooking Green Park in the fabulous frothy pink dining-room is a real treat (**£££**). ② **Le Caprice** (Arlington House). One of London's most fashionable and star-studded restaurants, informal yet punctilious, with the bonus of excellent food, reasonably priced (**££**). ③ **St James's Street**, gateway to clubland, a way of life un-ruffled by the feminist revolution where gentlemen reinforce their prejudices in com-fortable surroundings, including: ④ **Boodle's**. Members watch the world go by from the famous bay windows. ⑤ **Brooks's**. Once notorious for gambling. ⑥ **The Carlton**. Tory stronghold. ⑦ **Oxford and Cambridge Club** where women have a foothold. ⑧ **Army and Navy Club**. ⑨ The **Economist Building**, (No. 25), (A and P Smithson, 1964) suc-cessfully complements 18thC St James's. ⑩ **Stafford Hotel**. A club for those who don't have one and preferred by many who do. ⑪ **Spencer House**. A Palladian mansion by John Vardy recently completely restored and open on Sun. ⑫ **Dukes Hotel** upholds the best⁻traditions of St James's (**£££**). ⑬ Art dealers abound in and around **King Street**, notably Spink & Co (Nos 5-7), and one of the world's great auction houses, Christie's, at No. 8. ⑭ Shops providing gentlemen with the necessities of life include: **Lobb's**, (shoemak-ers of 9 St James's Street), **James Lock & Co**, (hatters, No. 6), **Berry Bros. & Rudd** (wine merchants, No. 3), and **House of Hardy** for fishing tackle (61 Pall Mall). ⑮ Nell Gwynn lived at **79 Pall Mall** and Gainsbo-rough died at **No. 82**, which is part of Schom-berg House, whose Queen Anne exterior has been preserved. ⑯ **St James's Palace** was built by Henry VIII on a human scale around four courts. The Gatehouse is the most strik-ing Tudor survivor. ⑰ **Chapel Royal** con-tinues its tradition of fine choral music. ⑱ The **Queen's Chapel** (Inigo Jones, 1627), the first English church in the classical style. ⑲ **Lancaster House**, now used for govern-ment receptions, was built for the Duke of York in 1827 by Benjamin Wyatt. ⑳ **Clarence House**, rebuilt by John Nash in 1828, is the home of the Queen Mother. ㉑ A charming **memorial to Queen Alexandra** by Sir Alfred Gilbert. ㉒ **Marlborough House**. Now the Commonwealth Secretariat, it was built for Sarah, Duchess of Marlborough by Wren in 1709-11.

Pall Mall/St James's Park

Admiralty Arch

THE MALL

Horse
Guards Parade

▶ 110

① **St James's Square**, centre-piece of London's most gentlemanly district, St James's. It was developed by the Earl of St Albans in the mid-17thC and has been a stamping ground of the upper crust ever since. ② **Pall Mall**, where the French game of *palle maile* was played with mallet and ball. When it became a fashionable boulevard, the name stuck. Known for its gentlemen's clubs whose splendid 19thC façades predominate. Here are ③ the **Junior Carlton Club**; ④ the **Royal Automobile Club** (with squash courts and elegant marble swimming-pool); ⑤ the **Reform Club** (classically clubby interior round an inner courtyard); ⑥ the **Travellers' Club** (lovely façade by Sir Charles Barry); and ⑦ Decimus Burton's stunning **Athenaeum**. ⑧ Its pair, now the **Institute of Directors**, is Nash, remodelled by Burton, but lacks the purity of the Athenaeum. ⑨ **Waterloo Place** (1816), the grand beginning of Nash's great route, via Regent Street, to Regent's Park. It started from Carlton House, the lavish home of the then Prince of Wales, who perversely had it demolished when he became George IV and decided to upgrade to Buckingham Palace. This Nash splendour is capped by ⑩ the **Duke of York's Column** (Benjamin Wyatt, 1831-4), approached by a broad flight of steps from the Mall. The Duke of York in question (statue by Sir Richard Westmacott) was the second son of George III and is best known today for the nursery rhyme about him. ⑪ Pristine **Carlton House Terrace** replaced Carlton House and was Nash's last work, resplendent, of course, in Doric column and gleaming stucco. ⑫ The **Institute of Contemporary Arts** (ICA) is an avant-garde arts (including film) centre. Vegetarian self-service restaurant (**£**). ⑬ The **Mall Galleries** exhibit traditional paintings. ⑭ When Sir Aston Webb refaced Buckingham Palace he also provided London with a much-needed processional route in **The Mall** (c1910). On Sundays it becomes a traffic-free promenade. ⑮ The central gates of Webb's massive **Admiralty Arch** (1911) open only for royal processions. ⑯ In summer, the creeper-covered **Citadel**, a wartime bomb shelter, resembles nothing so much as a giant hedge. ⑰ **St James's Park** has all one could wish for from a royal park; even pelicans descended from a pair given to Charles II. Made beautiful and fashionable by him, it was further improved by Nash, whose curving lake (lovely views from the bridge) attracts a rich birdlife.

Whitehall

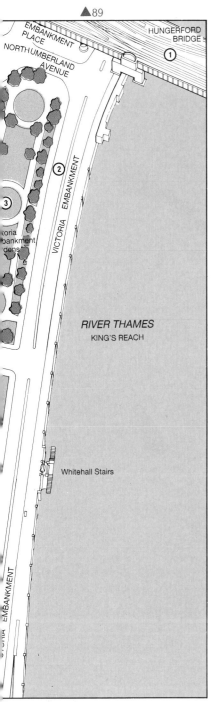

▲89

RIVER THAMES
KING'S REACH

Whitehall Stairs

▼129

① Though **Hungerford Bridge** (rail) flaunts its utilitarian ugliness, there are breathtaking views from its walkway. ② **Victoria Embankment**, part of Bazalgette's improvements (*see page 147*). ③ **Victoria Embankment Gardens** are dotted with statues and memorials; concerts on summer evenings. ④ **Whitehall**. Now synonymous with faceless bureaucrats, it is named after the Palace of Whitehall, seat of power of the Tudors and Stuarts. This wide route to Parliament is lined with government offices, powerhouses of civil servants and their ministers. ⑤ The façade of the **telephone exchange** in Craig's Court dates from 1702. ⑥ The 13thC **Silver Cross** is packed with civil servants from breakfast onwards. ⑦ **Old Admiralty** (1725), with a stone screen by Robert Adam. ⑧ **Ministry of Defence**. ⑨ **Royal Horseguards**, a Thistle hotel, moderately priced by London standards, with wonderful views over the river. ⑩ **Horse Guards**, by William Kent, is guarded by motionless troopers from the Household Division. (Mounting the guard takes place at 11.00 Mon-Sat, 10.00 Sun.) The building is best viewed from ⑪ the **Parade**. This ancient tournament ground, now ignominiously used as a car park, is restored to glory every June at the Trooping the Colour, which has honoured the monarch's official birthday since 1805. ⑫ **Banqueting House**, Inigo Jones's jewel of 1622. The only part of James I's proposed new palace to be built. It survived the fire of 1698 which destroyed the old palace. A startling building in its day, it is now somewhat dwarfed by the monoliths of Whitehall. The magnificent first-floor double cube-shaped room has a ceiling by Rubens glorifying James I. It was outside the Banqueting House that Charles I was executed, and inside that Charles II celebrated his restoration. Open Tue-Sun. ⑬ **Gwydyr House** (1722). The Welsh Office is one of the least intimidating of the ministries. ⑭ The **New Ministry of Defence** hides beneath it a cellar from Henry VIII's time; beside it are ⑮ **Queen Mary's Steps** which once led down to the river. ⑯ The **Cabinet Office** (1733-6; formerly the Treasury) is linked directly to ⑰ **10 Downing Street**, Prime Ministers' official residence since 1732. The Chancellor of the Exchequer lives at No. 11, and No. 12 is the Party Whips' office. ⑱ Every year on the Sunday nearest 11th November, the 'Glorious Dead' of two world wars are remembered in a solemn ceremony at Sir Edwin Lutyens's **Cenotaph**.

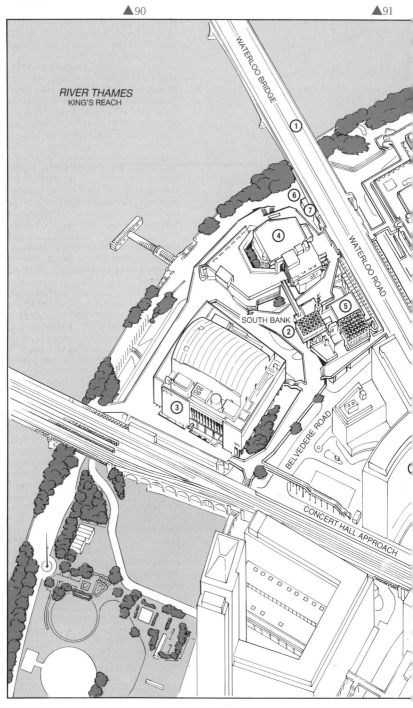

RIVER THAMES
KING'S REACH

WATERLOO BRIDGE

WATERLOO ROAD

SOUTH BANK

BELVEDERE ROAD

CONCERT HALL APPROACH

South Bank

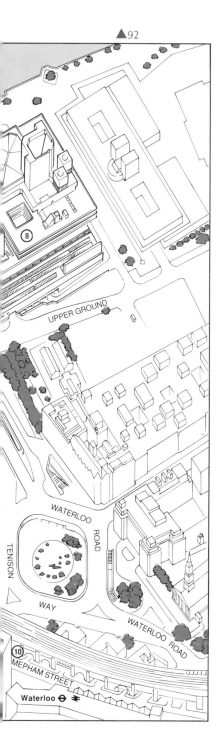

① **Waterloo Bridge**. In 1939 Sir Giles Gilbert Scott's smooth, cantilevered concrete bridge replaced the much praised original ('the noblest bridge in the world', according to the artist Canova, perhaps a touch over-enthusiastically) which was in danger of collapse. Designed by John Rennie and opened in 1817, it honoured the defeat of Napoleon at Waterloo two years earlier. ② **The South Bank Arts Centre** has been growing since 1951, when post-war London decided to buck itself up with the Festival of Britain (remember the Skylon Obelisk and the Dome of Discovery?). The semi-derelict Lambeth riverside was chosen for the exhibition site, and one permanent building was included amongst the temporary ones: the Festival Hall. Typical of post-war architecture, the complex presents something of a brutalist concrete jungle, and it is to undergo a major overhaul by architect Terry Farrell. Internally the buildings serve their purpose well, knitting together performance spaces with cafés, restaurants, bars, bookshops, galleries and terraces to create a vibrant hub for the arts in London. ③ **The Royal Festival Hall**, with later glass façade (1962-5), has a 3000-seat concert-hall and a complicated internal layout; alongside, under Hungerford Arches is the South Bank Craft Centre. ④ **The Queen Elizabeth Hall** and intimate **Purcell Room** (1967) are smaller-scale concert-halls. On an upper level ⑤ the **Hayward Gallery** provides space for major Arts Council exhibitions. Under Waterloo Bridge is ⑥ **The National Film Theatre**. Immediately behind, its red bubbled edges popping out on either side of Waterloo Bridge, is ⑦ the new **Museum of the Moving Image**, opened in September 1988, an exciting 'hands-on' gallop through the art of the moving image, from Chinese shadow theatre to film and TV techniques of the 21stC. ⑧ A National Theatre Company was first mooted 130 years before it finally took root at the **National Theatre** (Sir Denys Lasdun, 1970-6) with its mesh of useful interlocking spaces and three stages, the Olivier (open), Lyttelton (proscenium) and Cottesloe (courtyard). ⑨ The vast **Shell Centre** (1962) runs along Belvedere Road, named after Belvedere House and pleasure gardens which lay, in the 18thC, on the site of the Festival Hall. ⑩ **Drury Tea and Coffee Co** (1 Mepham Street). All sorts of teas, and 22 types of coffee roasted daily in a huge machine.

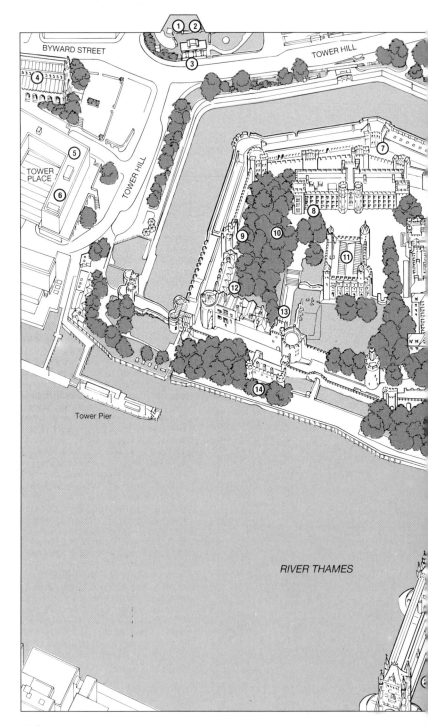

BYWARD STREET

TOWER HILL

TOWER HILL

TOWER PLACE

Tower Pier

RIVER THAMES

Tower of London

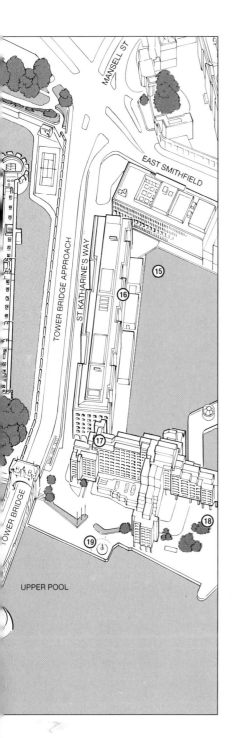

① Site of the scaffold on **Tower Hill** where prisoners (see 10) from the Tower were publicly executed. ② Maufe's 1939-45 **Mercantile Marine Memorial** in a sunken garden. ③ Lutyens's tunnel-vaulted pavilion, a 1914-18 war memorial. From here, the green copper roof and steeple of ④ **All Hallows-by-the-Tower** is visible. On the site of a Roman villa, the first church was Saxon. Rebuilt many times, most recently in 1949-58, it contains a magnificent font cover by Grinling Gibbons. ⑤ **Tower Place** (1962-5), concrete and glass pedestrian complex designed by Anthony Beckles Willson. ⑥ **Tiger Tavern**. A new pub on the site of an older one, it displays a mummified cat, supposedly befriended by Princess Elizabeth when she was a prisoner in the Tower. ⑦ **Tower of London**. Britain's most perfect and impregnable medieval fortress, begun by William I, functioned as a palace, a prison, the royal mint, a royal observatory and public records office. It still houses the priceless Crown Jewels in ⑧ **Waterloo Barracks**, guarded by the famous Beefeaters, and is home to six ravens. ⑨ Prisoners of rank were kept in **Beauchamp Tower**, where their carved graffiti survives. ⑩ **Tower Green**, site of the scaffold where prisoners of noble blood were privately executed. ⑪ The oldest building, the **White Tower**, so called after it was whitewashed by Henry III. Many prisoners languished in its dungeons, one of which, Little Ease, is just 4-feet-square. It also contains an armoury and a beautiful Norman chapel. ⑫ **Queen's House**, where Anne Boleyn spent her last days. ⑬ **Bloody Tower**, where the little princes were allegedly murdered. ⑭ **Traitors' Gate**, river entrance used for prisoners brought from Westminster. ⑮ Engineer Thomas Telford's **St Katharine's Dock**, opened in 1828, and the first of the docks to be redeveloped in the 1970s with shops, restaurants and a yacht marina. Telford's arcaded warehouses and Ivory House survive. Among the new buildings are ⑯ the **World Trade Centre** and ⑰ the sprawling but well-run **Tower Thistle Hotel**. ⑱ Site of the **Hospital of St Katharine**, founded by Queen Matilda in the 12thC. ⑲ Wynne's delightful **bronze fountain**, *Girl with a Dolphin*. ⑳ Decorative double-bascule **Tower Bridge** (1886-94), designed by engineer Sir John Wolfe-Barry and architect Sir Horace Jones. Its museum preserves the hydraulic machinery that operated the bridge before electrification in 1976.

Kensington
Gore

KENSINGTON RD

ALBERT HALL MANSIONS

EXHIBITION ROAD

Princes Gate

PRINCE CONSORT ROAD

Queen's Tower

▼132

South Kensington

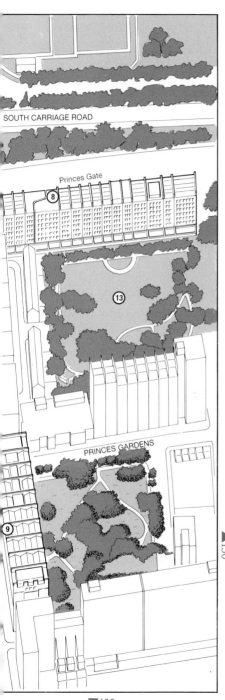

SOUTH CARRIAGE ROAD

Princes Gate

⑧

⑬

PRINCES GARDENS

⑨

▲130

(1) Self-effacing Prince Albert would not have wanted the **Albert Memorial** (1876), which stands in Kensington Gardens (*see page 101*), just west of where the Crystal Palace housed his Great Exhibition of 1851. In Sir George Gilbert Scott's version of a medieval shrine, a round-backed Albert reads an Exhibition catalogue under an enamel-, jewel- and mosaic-encrusted canopy, topped by a spire and surrounded by complex statuary. Undeniably ugly and endearingly over the top, the Memorial perfectly encapsulates the Victorian age. It surveys Albert's vision of a centre of culture and education, only realized, in part at least, after his untimely death in 1861. At present under wraps, awaiting restoration. Ringing the Albert Hall are: (2) the **Royal College of Organists**, like a piece of flashy costume jewellery with its mauve and blue sgraffito façade (1875); (3) **Memorial to the Great Exhibition**, with Albert aloft, of course; (4) turretted **Albert Court** (1890), with a novel entrance corridor, and (5) Norman Shaw's sweeping **Albert Hall Mansions** (c1880). (6) **The Royal Albert Hall** (c1870, by Fowke and Scott, who were engineers, not architects). Albert's crowning glory and London's favourite concert hall, annual venue of the famous Proms, as well as other diverse entertainments from boxing to beauty contests. (7) Looking like a displaced country house (it was a private home until 1912) the **Royal Geographical Society** is the work of Norman Shaw in mellow mood (1875). Its engrossing Map Room is open on weekdays. (8) 'Like tall thin gentlemen peering at something across the road' was how Leigh Hunt described the stucco terraces of **Princes Gate** (c1850). At No. 25 is the **Sikorski Museum** (open weekday afternoons) in the Polish Institute. South Kensington harbours a large, close-knit Polish community, many of whom patronize (9) **Ognisko Polskie** (The Polish Hearth Club; No. 55). Enjoy simple Polish fare in elegant surroundings amongst a charming mixture of bohemians, dignitaries and the occasional cassocked priest (**££**). (10) Visit the **Royal College of Music's** exquisite collection of instruments on a Mon or Wed in term time. (11) **Imperial College of Science and Technology**, part of London University, is made up of several Albert-inspired colleges. It was redeveloped in the 1960s, save the Queen's Tower (*see page 133*) and Sir Aston Webb's monumental Edwardian **School of Mines** on Prince Consort Road. (12) The **National Sound Archive** (No. 29; open weekdays). (13) Anyone can stroll across the lawn of **Princes Gardens**, owned by Imperial College.

▼133

117

HYDE PARK

NEW RIDE

SOUTH CARRIAGE DRIVE

Edinburgh Gate

KNIGHTSBRIDGE

Knightsbridge

KNIGHTSBRIDGE

GREEN

BROMPTON ROAD

LANCELOT PLACE

TREVOR SQUARE

BASIL STREET

SLOANE STREET

PAVILION ROAD

RYSBRACK ST

HANS CRESCENT

HANS ROAD

▲131

Harrods

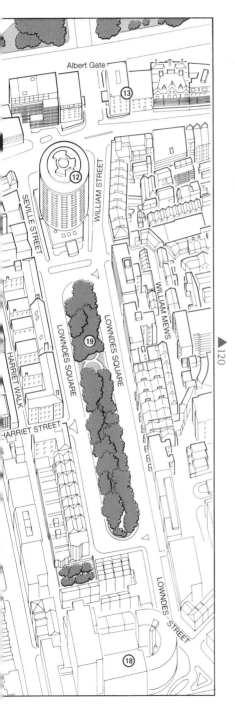

① **Knightsbridge** is the well-heeled shopper's paradise, with plenty of hotels and restaurants to revive flagging spirits. Harrods, besieged by chauffeured limousines, is the centre-piece, beckoning the dowagers, swathed in furs and poodles, from their expensive flats, and county ladies in town for a spending spree. ② **Hyde Park Barracks** (1967-70). Sir Basil Spence's 320ft tower, home of the Household Cavalry, disturbs the skyline. ③ **Mr Chow** (No. 151), 1960s sensation that gave Chinese food a sophisticated image (£££). ④ **Knightsbridge Green** is a reminder that this was once a country village. The stocks and maypole stood on the site of ⑤ the **Scotch House** (No. 2), famous emporium of cashmere and tartan. ⑥ Fleeing beneath Bowater House is Epstein's bronze group *Pan*, his last work (1959). ⑦ **Basil Street Hotel** where location, price and old-fashioned courtesy ensure that guests keep returning. ⑧ **The Stockpot** (No. 6). Cheerful, busy restaurant, popular with office workers, (£). ⑨ **Sloane Street**, smart shopping street linking Knightsbridge and Chelsea. ⑩ **Harvey Nichols** rivals Harrods for women's fashions and now boasts a trendy fifth floor café. ⑪ **Hyde Park Hotel**, an Edwardian palace favoured in those days by all visiting heads of state, and still bearing up well. Breakfasters have a grand view of the cavalry trotting down Rotten Row. **Marco Pierre White**, the much-vaunted chef, has his new restaurant here. ⑫ **The Sheraton Park Tower**: the higher up the better the room and the view. ⑬ The **French Embassy** was built by Thomas Cubitt for the railway millionaire George Hudson, who later went bust. ⑭ **Richoux** (No. 80) serves delicious sticky teas (££). ⑮ **Harrods**. The world's most famous store, by Stevens & Munt (1901-5), grew from a humble grocer's shop. Leaving your dog in the kennels you can arrange a funeral, take books out of the library, have your hair done, marvel at the sculptured wet fish display in the art deco Food Halls, spend, spend, spend, and recover in one of the six restaurants and five bars. ⑯ The **Capital**, a luxurious, intimate hotel with a romantic French restaurant (£££). ⑰ **L'Hotel**. The Capital's baby sister is a sophisticated 'bed and breakfast' with a good bistro, **Le Metro**, in the basement (££). ⑱ The **Hyatt Carlton Tower** is a favourite hotel of discerning jet-set travellers. Facilities include a tennis court. ⑲ **Lowndes Square** was built by Thomas Cubitt during the 1830s and 1840s as part of Belgravia (*see page 121*), and remains a very smart address.

119

Belgrave Square

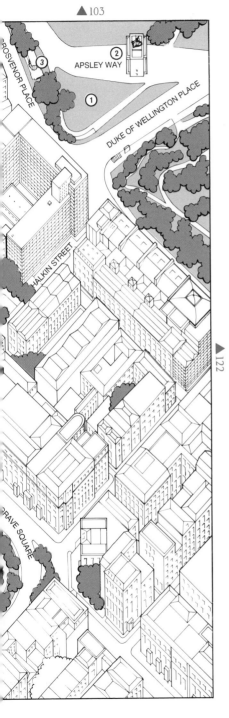

① **Hyde Park Corner** (*see also page 103*), once the western entrance to London, was conceived in the early 19thC as a triumphal approach from Buckingham Palace to Hyde Park. Today it is London's busiest round-about, its monuments hopelessly marooned by roaring traffic. ② **Constitution Arch** designed by Decimus Burton in 1828, is graced by Captain Adrian Jones's magnificent *Quadriga* (1912) depicting the Goddess of Peace quelling the four Horses of War. ③ The dramatic **Royal Artillery Monument** (C.S. Jaeger, 1920). ④ The former St George's Hospital is now the luxury American-owned **Lanesborough Hotel**. ⑤ The **Berkeley Hotel**, complete with roof-top pool, is one of London's most exclusive. ⑥ **Kinnerton Street**, nowadays a great deal more desirable than the slum, complete with open sewer, it once was. ⑦ **Salloos** (No. 62), authentic and excellent Pakistani cooking in a highly civil-ized setting (£££). ⑧ The cosy **Nag's Head**. ⑨ **St Paul's Knightsbridge** has a beautifully decorated interior. ⑩ the **Grenadier**, charming if touristy pub with military knick-knacks and a sentry box outside. ⑪ **Wilton Crescent** (W.H. Seth-Smith, 1827) makes a grand entrance from the north to Belgravia. The north side was refaced in stone early this century. ⑫ **Caledonian Club** (No. 9), for Scottish gentlemen or those with a close Hibernian association. ⑬ **Belgrave Square** is the centre-piece of Belgravia, the later of 2nd Earl of Grosvenor's two prestigious estates, the first being Mayfair (*see page 81*). The brilliantly successful developer Thomas Cubitt, was mainly responsible for the grand white stucco squares and terraces which grew up on marshland here from the 1820s to 1850s. (Cubitt was entirely responsible for Pimlico, later sold off by the Grosvenor Estate.) George Basevi was the architect of Belgrave Square, now mainly embassies. In the centre are nearly ten acres of private gar-dens. ⑭ In rarefied **Motcomb Street**, the cream-painted Doric columns of the Pan-technicon loom large. Once a huge ware-house and stabling complex, said to be fire-proof, it was burnt down in 1874 leaving only the façade. Opposite is ⑮ **Halkin Arcade**, with a façade dating, like the Pantechnicon, from the 1830s. ⑯ The **Turk's Head** and ⑰ the **Star Tavern** (6 Belgrave Mews West) are two more typical Belgravia pubs, with open fires and a cosy atmosphere.

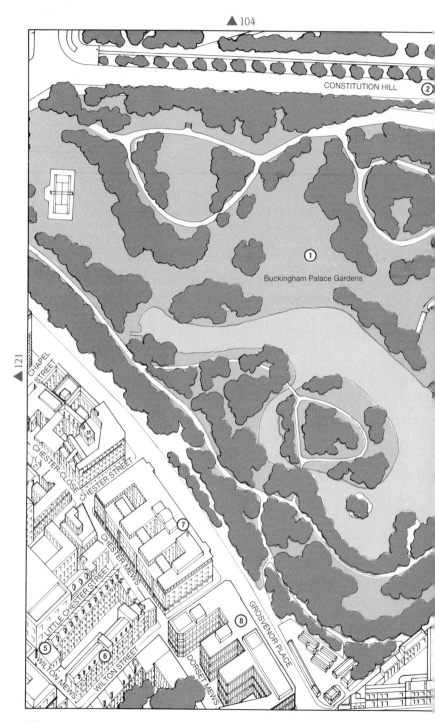

▲ 104

CONSTITUTION HILL

Buckingham Palace Gardens

CHAPEL STREET

▲ 121

CHESTER CLOSE

CHESTER STREET

CHESTER MEWS

CHESTER STREET

LITTLE CHESTER STREET

WILTON MEWS

WILTON STREET

GROSVENOR PLACE

DORSET MEWS

Constitution Hill/Royal Mews

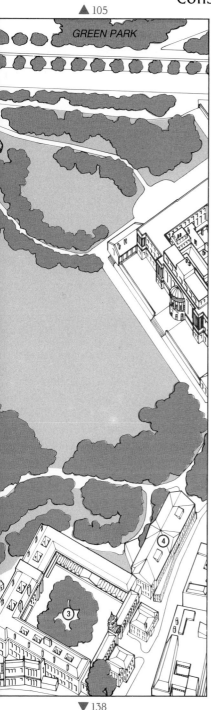

▲ 105

GREEN PARK

▶ 124

(1) Only very tall or very important people get to see the **gardens of Buckingham Palace**. The former may glimpse the tennis-courts from the top of passing buses, while the latter might be invited to one of the Queen's three annual garden parties. Below the Palace terrace stretches the immaculate lawn, judiciously planted with trees to screen it from prying eyes in the high-rise blocks that are springing up nearby. The lawn sweeps down to a three-acre lake – a noted haven for wildlife, including flamingos. Ornaments in the garden include the Waterloo Vase, standing 15ft high. Carved out of a single piece of Carrera marble, it was supposedly commissioned by Napoleon. The royal 45-acre back garden would be spectacular anywhere, but its position in the heart of London makes it unique.
(2) **Constitution Hill**. Lined by trees and old lamp-posts, its peaceful quality is marred by roaring through traffic. It was here in 1850 that Sir Robert Peel was thrown from his horse with fatal consequences after visiting the Palace. (3) **The Royal Mews** is architecturally the best bit of Buckingham Palace (*see page 125*) – unadulterated Nash. On Wed and Thur afternoons the public can see the fabulous royal carriages and cars. The stars of the show are the Gold State Coach made for George III in 1762 and always used for coronations, and the Glass State Coach which whisks fairy-tale princesses to their weddings.
(4) **The Riding House** was built in 1763-6, with a later frieze and pediment depicting a delightfully spirited *Hercules and the Thracian Horses*. (5) **The Grouse and Claret** (14-15 Little Chester Street), classical English food in a quiet pubby restaurant (**££**). (6) Henry Gray, author of *Gray's Anatomy*, the definitive medical textbook, lived at **8 Wilton Street** from 1827 until his death from smallpox in 1861. (7) Two large unedifying buildings occupy this stretch of Grosvenor Gardens. The first, currently the **Postal Headquarters**, was built in 1956. Its frieze depicts the forces of light triumphing over the forces of darkness. The other is (8) **Hobart House**, headquarters of British Coal.

▼ 138

▲106

Queen Victoria Memorial Gardens

THE MALL

CONSTITUTION HILL

Queen Victoria Memorial

Queen Victoria Memorial Gardens

③

① Buckingham Palace

▲123

②

BIRDCAGE WALK

BUCKINGHAM GATE

BUCKINGHAM GATE

STAFFORD PLACE

CATHERINE PLACE

CATHERINE PLACE

BUCKINGHAM PLACE

WILFRED ST

PALACE STREET

STAG PLACE

CASTLE LANE

124

▼138 ▼139

Buckingham Palace

▲ 107

St James's
Park Lake

ST JAMES'S PARK

BIRDCAGE WALK

► 126

PETTY FRANCE

BUCKINGHAM GATE

CAXTON STREET

① In its perfect setting at the bottom of the Mall, **Buckingham Palace** should be a dazzling glory of a building. In fact, the Queen's primary residence is, though stately, very dull. Still, it is the focus of the British monarchy and perhaps the single most stared at building in London. Built as a mansion for the Duke of Buckingham in 1703, it became the family home of George III and Queen Charlotte, and was later aggrandized for his son George IV by architect John Nash. Of all Nash's London schemes, this was his most problematic, and deep troubles over the finances left him disgraced at the end of an otherwise brilliant life. What we see today, however, is not the work of Nash, but of Edwardian architect Sir Aston Webb who, as well as creating Admiralty Arch and the Mall, put a new face on the palace. When the Queen is at home, the flag flies. The changing of the Guard takes place daily at 11.30 in summer, alternate days in winter. In order to raise money to pay for the restoration of Windsor Castle after its devastating fire, and to appear less aloof from her subjects, the Queen has now opened the Palace's State rooms to the public during the summer season. ② The **Queen's Gallery** was set up by Her Majesty in 1963 for the public to view changing selections from the incredibly rich and varied royal art collections. Always worth a visit. ③ Designed by Webb, sculpted by Sir Thomas Brock (1911), the **Victoria Memorial** livens up the view from the Mall of Webb's much more mundane palace front. A fittingly sentimental tribute to the Victorian age and its extraordinary queen. ④ The **Guards Museum** at **Wellington Barracks** (closed Sun; *see page 127*) traces the history of the Foot Guards, covering both their fighting and ceremonial roles. ⑤ **St James's Court**, late-Victorian, but expensively refurbished in heavy Edwardian style as the London flagship of the Taj hotel group. ⑥ 'Little France' got its name when French wool and cloth merchants lived here in the 16thC. The Passport Office is at Nos 70-78 **Petty France**. ⑦ **Blewcoat School** is now the **National Trust Shop and Information Centre**. As depicted by the statue of the blue-coated, shy-looking young boy on the front, it was built – in the early 18thC – as a charity school for local poor children. It closed and fell into disrepair until rescued by the National Trust in 1954.

125

▲108

St James's Park Lake

ST JAMES'S PARK

BIRDCAGE WA

②

⑥

OLD QUEEN

BIRDCAGE WALK

⑨

⑦

QUEEN ANNE'S GATE

⑧

⑤

▲125

③

④

QUEEN ANNE'S GATE

CARTERET STREET

DARTMOUTH ST

TOTHILL STREET

PETTY FRANCE

⊖ St James's Park

⑯

BROADWAY

⑱

⑲

⑳

New Scotland Yard

⑰

BROADWAY

VICTORIA STREET

㉑

Birdcage Walk

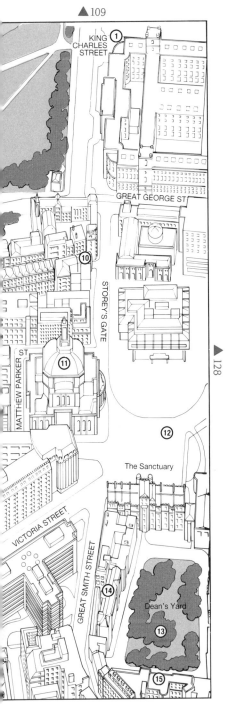

▲ 109

KING
CHARLES
STREET

GREAT GEORGE ST

STOREY'S GATE

MATTHEW PARKER ST

▶ 128

The Sanctuary

VICTORIA STREET

GREAT SMITH STREET

Dean's Yard

① In King Charles Street (Clive of India faces St James's Park) is the entrance to the **Cabinet War Rooms**. Though tucked away, Churchill's wartime bunker, laid out as it was then, is well worth a visit (closed Mon). ② **Birdcage Walk** was lined with Charles II's aviaries. Opposite the park are the little gardens and pretty bowed backs of the 18thC houses in Queen Anne's Gate. ③ **The Guards Chapel**, attached to Wellington Barracks (*see page 125*), is a modern replacement for the one destroyed by a bomb with great loss of life in 1944. ④ The **Home Office**. ⑤ Set in a lush garden behind wrought-iron gates, **Queen Anne's Mews** must be the prettiest (private) car park in London. ⑥ **Cockpit Stairs** commemorate the 18thC Royal Cockpit which stood here. They lead up to ⑦ **Queen Anne's Gate**. With Old Queen Street, this is a miraculously preserved 18thC enclave of stone-striped, brown-brick houses (now decorous offices), each with an attractive doorway. Lord Palmerston was born at No. 20. ⑧ A statue of a demure-looking **Queen Anne** marks the place where a wall once divided the street into two closes. ⑨ The **Two Chairmen**, a quaint corner pub established in 1756. ⑩ **Westminster Arms**, popular lunch-time local with a Division Bell. ⑪ **Methodist Central Hall** (1911). ⑫ **Broad Sanctuary**, so named because of the long-gone Sanctuary Tower which once gave refuge to fugitives. ⑬ **Dean's Yard**, entered through an archway in Sir George Gilbert Scott's Gothic offices (1854), contains ⑭ **Westminster Abbey Choir School** and ⑮ **Church House**. ⑯ **Broadway House** (No. 55) is the headquarters of London Transport (information centre). A 1920s pile, its stone figures of *Night and Day* are by Jacob Epstein, with reliefs by Eric Gill and Henry Moore amongst others. ⑰ **Memorial**, in the form of a bronze scroll, to the struggle of the suffragettes. ⑱ **Stakis St Ermin's**, traditional hotel with much of its late-Victorian character still intact. ⑲ **Villa Claudius**, Italian restaurant where live opera is performed Mon-Fri evenings (No. 10a; **£££**) with an intriguing entrance in front of ⑳ **New Scotland Yard**, the Metropolitan Police headquarters. ㉑ The elongated **Department of Trade and Industry**.

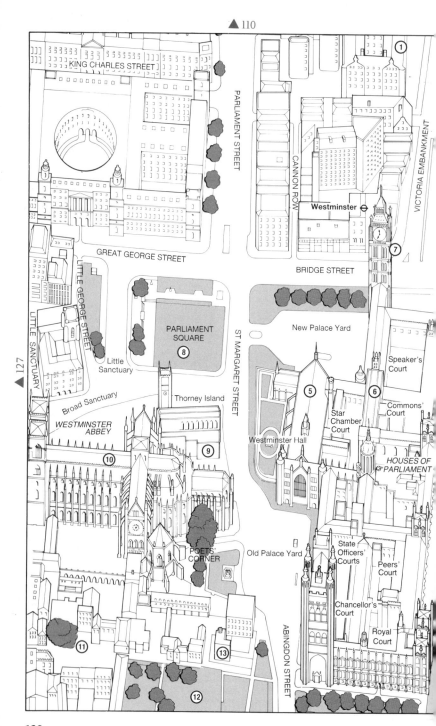

▲110

KING CHARLES STREET

PARLIAMENT STREET

CANNON ROW

VICTORIA EMBANKMENT

①

Westminster ⊖

⑦

GREAT GEORGE STREET

BRIDGE STREET

▲127

LITTLE GEORGE STREET

LITTLE SANCTUARY

PARLIAMENT SQUARE

⑧

New Palace Yard

ST MARGARET STREET

Little Sanctuary

Speaker's Court

⑥

Broad Sanctuary

Thorney Island

⑤

Star Chamber Court

Commons' Court

WESTMINSTER ABBEY

⑩

⑨

Westminster Hall

HOUSES OF PARLIAMENT

POETS' CORNER

Old Palace Yard

State Officers' Courts

Peers' Court

⑪

Chancellor's Court

Royal Court

⑬

ABINGDON STREET

⑫

128

Houses of Parliament

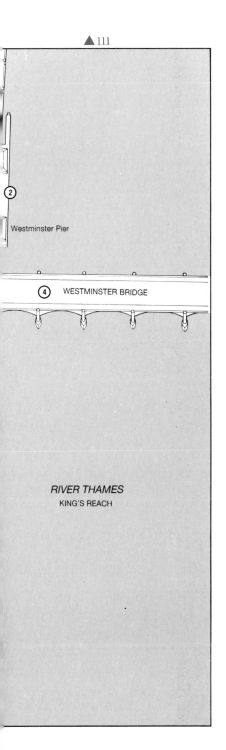

▲ 111

② Westminster Pier

WESTMINSTER PIER

④ WESTMINSTER BRIDGE

RIVER THAMES
KING'S REACH

① The **Norman Shaw building** (1886-90; formerly New Scotland Yard), a baroque castle with a hint of the Highlands. ② **Westminster Pier**, starting point for boat trips on the Thames. ③ Fierce **Queen Boudicca** and her daughters are immortalized in full battle cry in Thomas Thornycroft's bronze. ④ **Westminster Bridge**, perennially favoured viewpoint for photographs. ⑤ Part of the New Palace of Westminster (official title of the Houses of Parliament), **Westminster Hall** dates from 1097, with considerable alterations in the 14thC including the fabulous oak hammer-beam roof. The original Palace of Westminster was home to the monarchy from the 11thC until Henry VIII moved to Whitehall. ⑥ After a fire in 1834, Sir Charles Barry and Augustus Pugin were commissioned to build the **Houses of Parliament** (containing, most notably, the House of Commons and the House of Lords). ⑦ London's best-loved landmark, **Big Ben** has, like the rest of the Palace of Westminster, been restored to its full Gothic splendour. ⑧ The statues of statesmen and heroes in **Parliament Square** are besieged by thundering traffic. Winston Churchill (Ivor Robert-Jones, 1973), remains indomitable. ⑨ **St Margaret's**. The parish church of the House of Commons always attracts star-spotters for weddings and christenings. Much rebuilt since the 12thC, it includes lovely windows by John Piper (1967). ⑩ **Westminster Abbey**. Edward the Confessor established the first great church and monastery on this site – once a swamp – but the present abbey dates from Henry III's time when, in 1245, he conceived the idea of this magnificent stage for coronations and royal burials. Building continued over the centuries, including Henry VII's chapel (1503-12), a miracle of the stonemason's art; and the West Towers by Wren (1745). The memorials to the great and good (and to some who just paid for them) are so numerous that they obscure some of the beauty of the interior, and a sacred atmosphere is hard to maintain given the sheer number of visitors. ⑪ **Little Dean's Yard** contains the main buildings of Westminster School – the dining-room dates from the 1360s. ⑫ The **Abbey Garden** is the fruit of 900 years of cultivation. ⑬ The **Jewel Tower** (1365-6; open to public) is part of the original Palace of Westminster and used to house the king's treasures.

ENNISMORE GARDENS

ENNISMORE GARDENS

ENNISMORE MEWS

RUTLAND GATE

RUTLAND GATE

MONTPELIER WALK

ENNISMORE STREET

COTTAGE PLACE

BROMPTON SQUARE

THURLOE PLACE

BROMPTON ROAD

EGERTON GARDENS

NORTH TERRACE

Brompton Road

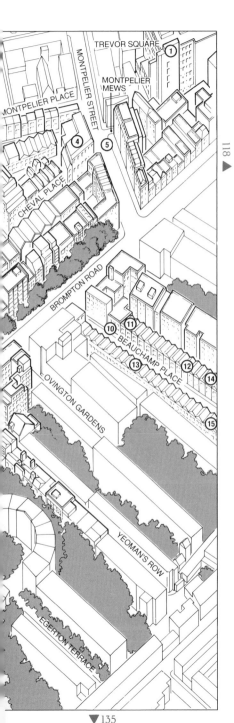

118

① In 1913, **Harrods** built its **warehouse** and garage on the site of slums in Trevor Square. Tunnels connect the warehouse with the shop (*see page 149*). ② **Ennismore Arms**, cosy pub in a pretty cobbled mews. ③ Grooming posts still stand in **Ennismore Street**. ④ **Bonhams** (Montpelier Galleries), auctioneers since 1793; good for paintings, furniture, rugs, wine and the odd bargain. ⑤ Until the 1890s, the **Montpelier Street** area was a working-class one, hence the proliferation of pubs. ⑥ T.L. Donaldson's Victorian-Gothic **Holy Trinity Church**. ⑦ Horseshoe-shaped **Brompton Square** (early 19thC) is one of the prettiest in London. ⑧ **Brompton Road** follows the original track from Knightsbridge to the hamlet of Broom Farm (Brompton). ⑨ **Bunch of Grapes**, authentic Victorian pub, complete with snob screens. ⑩ Pretty but pricey, **Beauchamp Place** is packed with chic fashion boutiques, including ⑪ **Janet Reger** (No. 2), for sexy silk underwear, ⑫ **Caroline Charles** (No. 11) for a classic look, **Bruce Oldfield** (No. 27, off map) for stunning evening wear, and ⑬ **Beauchamp Place Shop** (No. 55) for a host of designer labels. ⑭ Starters and puddings only are served at **Ménage à Trois** (No. 15; **£££**); delectable but tiny portions. ⑮ Sit back on a Chesterfield and admire the military prints at the **Grove Tavern** (No. 43). Spot the famous faces at glitzy Italian restaurant **San Lorenzo** (No. 22, off map; **£££**). ⑯ Set up after the Great Exhibition of 1851 and covering 100 acres, the **Victoria and Albert** is one of the world's greatest museums of decorative art (*see page 133*). ⑰ Herbert Gribble's extravagant baroque **London Oratory** of St Philip Neri (1878-84), the first important Roman Catholic church to be built after the Reformation. ⑱ With its wood-panelled walls, linen tablecloths and waiters in white aprons, **St Quentin** (No. 243; **££**) feels like a real Parisian brasserie (open every day). ⑲ Around the corner, sister restaurant **Grill St Quentin** (2 Yeoman's Row; **££**) dispenses steak and chips, French-style. ⑳ **Rembrandt Hotel**, in business since the turn of the century, but now totally modernized.

South Kensington/Cromwell Road

▲ 117

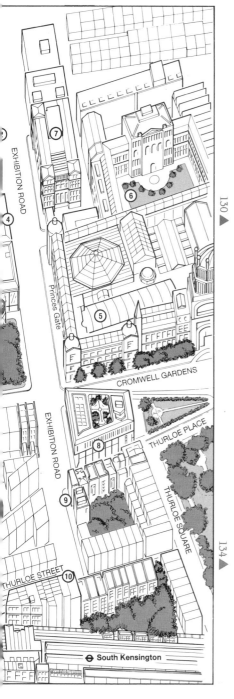

① **Queen's Tower** (*see page 117*) provides splendid views from its top (conducted tours Jul-Oct). ② The department store format of Sir Richard Allison's **Science Museum** (1913) serves its purpose well. Determined to keep up with the times, the museum has recently been revamped and includes popular new exhibitions such as Exploration of Space and the Launch Pad for children. ③ The splendid entrance of the **Natural History Museum**, vast offshoot of the British Museum, lies on an invisible axis with the Royal Albert Hall, marking out the area of museums and colleges nicknamed 'Albertopolis' (*see page 117*). Alfred Waterhouse's Romanesque cathedral to natural science (1873-81) has an impressive stone and terracotta striped frontage alive with animals. Inside, the great iron-roofed nave and long side wings house 500,000 items of zoology, botany, palaeontology, mineralogy and entomology, dominated by the dinosaur Diplodocus in the central hall. Pick your subjects, or interest can flag. ④ The ex-Geological Museum was a latecomer in 1935, though founded in 1837, and was rather lost between its giant siblings. It is now known as the **Earth Galleries** of the Natural History Museum, and is linked to the latter by a corridor. Worth visiting for its gems and the adventurous Story of the Earth display. ⑤ **The Victoria and Albert Museum**, known to all as the V & A, is the world's largest museum of decorative arts, a wonderfully rich pot-pourri of treasures. So vast is the museum's hoard – from the Great Bed of Ware to the music room of a St James's town house, from the entire contents of the old India Museum to the Raphael Cartoons – that thousands of priceless objects lie mouldering in store-rooms for lack of space. The building itself evolved falteringly from 1856 until 1909 when Sir Aston Webb's glowering façade sealed its identity. Highlights are the beautifully decorated original refreshment rooms, the Italianate terracotta façade of ⑥ **the quadrangle** (Pirelli Garden) and ⑦ the **Henry Cole Wing**. Built in 1863-73, this was incorporated into the museum in 1984 (it contains the lovely Constable Collection) and commemorates its first and greatest director. Go to the V & A prepared to get hopelessly lost, but never bored. ⑧ The **Ismaili Centre** (Sir Hugh Casson, 1983). Of the museums, only the V&A provides decent food. Alternatively try ⑨ **Paper Tiger** (Nos 10-12) for Szechuan cooking (**££**); **Gilberts** (No. 2) for modern British cooking in a popular local restaurant (**££**); or better still, ⑩ **Daquise** (No. 20) a Polish café/restaurant delightfully frozen in time (**£**).

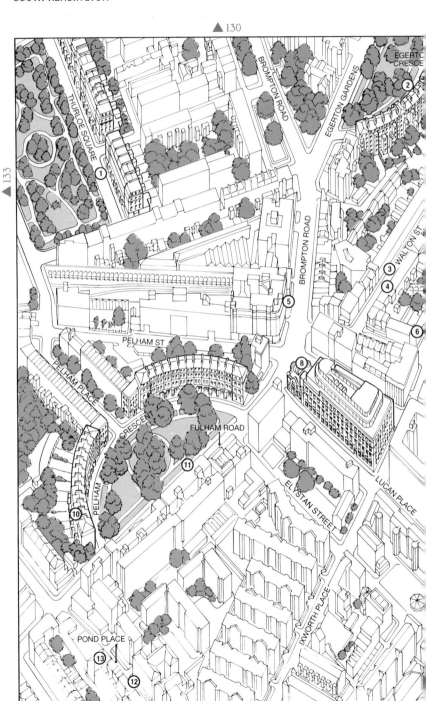

▲ 130

◄ 133

THURLOE SQUARE

BROMPTON ROAD

EGERTON GARDENS

EGERTON CRESCE

②

BROMPTON ROAD

WALTON ST.

③

④

⑤

⑥

①

PELHAM ST

⑧

PELHAM PLACE

PELHAM CRESCENT

PELHAM

FULHAM ROAD

⑪

ELYSTAN STREET

LUCAN PLACE

⑩

IXWORTH PLACE

POND PLACE

⑬

⑫

▼ 142

Fulham Road/Sloane Avenue

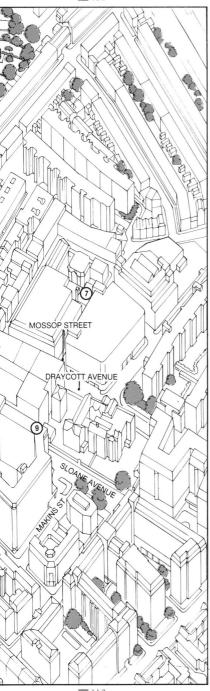

① **Thurloe Square** (1843): elegant brick and stucco houses by George Basevi surround a tranquil tree-filled garden. ② **Egerton Crescent** is on a grander scale, and was commissioned by Smith's Charity Estate, whose trustees developed the area when the original beneficiaries (Christian prisoners of North African pirates) were thin on the ground. ③ **Walton Street**, charming and narrow, is worth strolling down for its diverse shops, art galleries and restaurants, including ④ the intimate **Ma Cuisine** (No. 113; **£££**) and Italian **San Martino** (No. 103; **££**). ⑤ Glossy, French **La Brasserie** (No. 272) for light meals and lazy breakfasts with the papers (**££**). ⑥ **Le Suquet** (104 Draycott Avenue), authentic French seafood restaurant; *plateau de fruits de mer* is the crowning glory (**£££**). ⑦ A haunt of young Chelsea is the **Admiral Codrington** (Mossop Street) which, unusually, has a large garden. ⑧ **Michelin House**, magnificent and superbly restored art deco landmark, now the elegant Conran Shop, plus an oyster bar (ground floor) and **Bibendum**, Terence Conran's beautifully designed restaurant, with equally impressive food by Simon Hopkinson (**£££**; first floor). ⑨ Two diverse restaurants in Chelsea Cloisters: **Albero and Grana** (**£££**) serving Spanish style combinations, and long running **Zen**, now rather soulless and very Westernized Chinese (**£££**). ⑩ Sir Nigel Playfair, actor-manager, lived at **26 Pelham Crescent**, one of Basevi's white stucco houses which sweep gently round the immaculate private gardens. ⑪ Now stylish, this stretch of the Fulham Road, opposite Pelham Crescent, is lined with specialist shops which include jewellers and watchmakers, and also **The Sleeping Company** (linens), **Divertimenti** (kitchenware), **Agnès B** French separates for men and women) and **Smallbone of Devizes** designer kitchens, impressively sited in The Old Chelsea Glass Company offices. ⑫ **Pond Place** marks the route beasts took to the ponds of Chelsea Common, built over in the late 18thC.

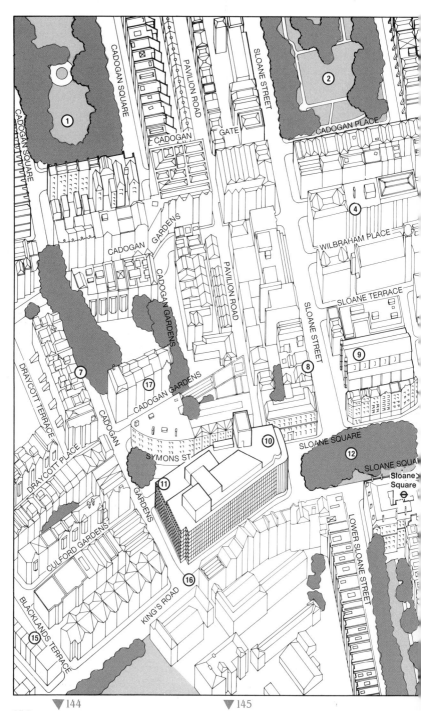

Sloane Square

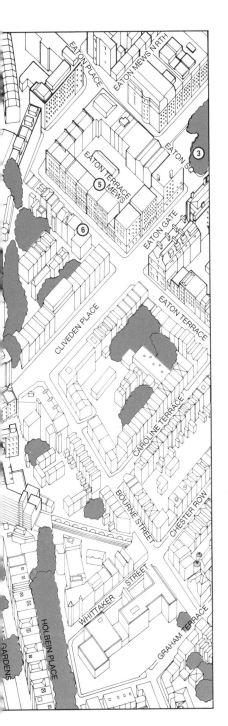

(1) An early red-brick development, innovative after so much white stucco, **Cadogan Square** (1876-90), is the heart of the impressive Cadogan Estate; begun when Elizabeth Cadogan, Baroness Oakley, inherited the Sloane estates from her father, Sir Hans Sloane. (2) **Cadogan Place**, tall, gleaming, white houses overlooking spacious private gardens. (3) Across Sloane Street and into Belgravia (*see page 121*), **Eaton Square** is perhaps London's most prestigious address. (4) The **Wilbraham** (No. 1): a genteel hotel with fair prices. (5) **Eaton Terrace Mews** typifies Belgravia's many charming mews (formerly stables and coach-houses). (6) **The Antelope**, pretty 18thC pub with a hearty clientele. (7) **Fenja** (No. 69), a small, elegant town house hotel. (8) A cluster of shops to keep Sloane Rangers happy in this section of Sloane Street include the **General Trading Company** (GTC: No. 144), their ultimate store; **Jane Churchill** (No. 135), their favourite mix n' match decorator shop; **Partridges** (Nos 132-134), upmarket delicatessen and supermarket; and **Coles** (No. 131) where they buy their shirts. (9) The interior of **Holy Trinity** (J.D. Sedding, 1888-90) is an Arts and Crafts delight. The fine east window, for example, was designed by Burne-Jones and made by William Morris and Company. (10) Like its brother department store, John Lewis (*see page 61*) Londoners find **Peter Jones** indispensable. Quite justifiably the John Lewis motto is 'never knowingly undersold'. A model building, too (1936). Notice, on the corner of Symons Street, the idiosyncratic windows of (11) **No. 25**, designed tongue-twistingly by A.H. Mackmurdo for Mortimer Mempes in 1893. (12) **Sloane Square**, undistinguished in itself, is a focal point and draws together the edges of Chelsea, Knightsbridge, Belgravia and Pimlico. (13) **Oriel** (No. 50); crowded brasserie best for snacks such as *croque monsieur* (**££**). (14) **Royal Court Theatre**, home of the English Stage Company, who started with a bang in 1956 with *Look Back in Anger*. (15) One of the best small bookshops in London, **John Sandoe** (No. 10) is patronized by well-known readers and writers alike. (16) Chelsea's bohemian streak still finds expression in the **King's Road**, long after the Swinging Sixties made it famous. Respectable locals mingle with outlandish incomers, especially on Saturdays, and colour and life abound. The road began as a private thoroughfare to Hampton Court for Charles II; all other travellers had to produce a special copper pass. (17) **Draycott Hotel** (No. 24), another of the sophisticated house-hotels which are tempting even stars away from more impersonal establishments.

137

▲ 123

Victoria

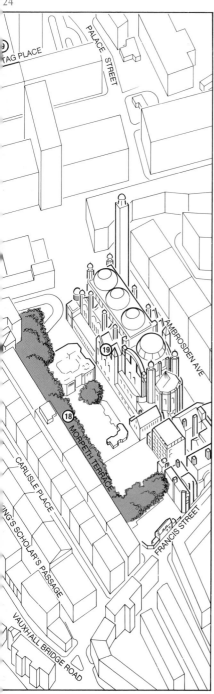

① **The Goring Hotel**, still owned by the descendants of the first, eponymous, proprietor and still noted for its traditional approach. ② Tiny **Victoria Square** is an unexpectedly elegant corner amidst the anonymous bustle of Victoria. ③ Once prey to highwaymen, **Buckingham Palace Road** is today an unexciting thoroughfare. At its northern end are: ④ equestrian book specialist **J.A. Allen** (1 Lower Grosvenor Place); ⑤ **Carriages** (No. 43), a civilized wine bar (**££**); ⑥ **Bumbles** (No. 16) a popular lunch spot (**££**); ⑦ the **Royal Westminster**, one of the reliable Thistle group's more luxurious hotels; and ⑧ **Transalpino** (No. 71), youth travel specialists. ⑨ The mighty aluminium **stag** (E. Bainbridge Copnall, 1962) recalls the once famous Stag Brewery which stood here from the 17thC until redevelopment in 1959. ⑩ The equestrian **statue of Marshall Foch** was presented by the French government along with the two square buildings encrusted with Normandy sea shells. ⑪ **Overtons** (4 Victoria Buildings, Terminus Place), traditional fish restaurant and oyster bar (**££**). ⑫ Built in the 1850s by architect H.R. Abraham, **Victoria Street** was noted for the even scale of its six-storey Italianate buildings. Today hardly an original building stands, and the street is lined with post-war edifices of varying degrees of mediocrity. ⑬ The **Victoria Palace**, built as a music-hall in 1911. ⑭ **The Grosvenor**, modest railway hotel with a typically overbearing Victorian façade. ⑮ **Victoria Station**, built in 1862. Constantly crowded with travellers to and from the south, the Continent and Gatwick, the station gives this part of Westminster its unsettled, transitory feel. In the forecourt is London's largest tourist information centre. ⑯ A thoroughly untheatrical exterior belies the splendidly garish interior of the **Apollo Victoria Theatre**, transformed in 1983 to house the musical *Starlight Express*. ⑰ **Costa Coffee Boutique** (No. 324); 22 types of coffee on sale, plus a small café. ⑱ **Morpeth Terrace** (1890s) was one of London's first purpose-built blocks of flats. Many of Victoria's mansion flats are home to MPs. ⑲ **Westminster Cathedral** is a highly original Byzantine basilica (J.F. Bentley, 1895-1903) with a peculiar striped cladding of brick and Portland stone. The interior decoration has, due to cost, never been finished, but there is an abundance of beautiful marble and, in the side chapels, glittering mosaic. Don't miss Eric Gill's reliefs in the nave, **The Stations of the Cross**. For an easily won birds'-eye view over London, take the lift (in summer) to the top of the campanile.

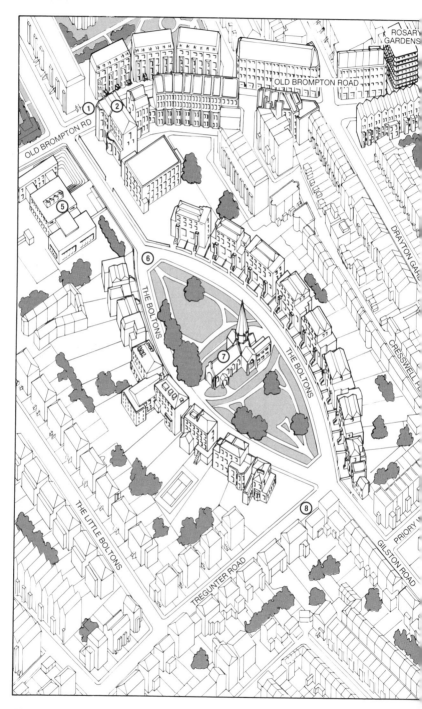

The Boltons

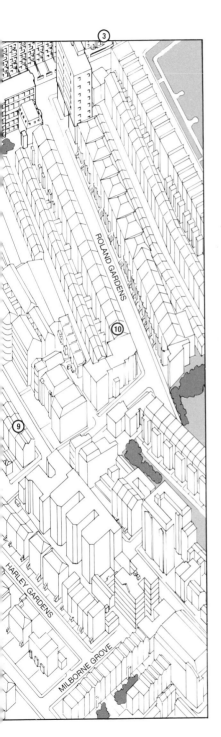

① In the 19thC, the **Old Brompton Road** wound its way through market gardens and nurseries, and this rural scene is recalled by the numerous 'Gardens' in the area. ② **No. 189** was the home of the soprano Jenny Lind, 'the Swedish Nightingale'. ③ Two restaurants in the stretch of Old Brompton Road between here and South Kensington Tube station are **Bar Escoba** (No. 102), London's best-known *tapas* bar (**££**); and **Hilaire** (No. 68) for high-flying modern British food (**£££**). ④ **Rosary Gardens**, named after a house which stood nearby. ⑤ **Bousfield Primary School**, built on the site of Beatrix Potter's home, won an architectural award in 1956. ⑥ **The Boltons**: these imposing twin crescents, built by George Godwin between 1850 and 1860, contain the most prized of the houses in this exclusive and secluded residential area, a bastion of English family life. With their large gardens front and back, they are still mostly single dwellings; the anglophile Douglas Fairbanks Jnr was once a resident. Although atypical of the London square, The Boltons illustrates the intimate, villagey atmosphere achieved by such an inward-facing design, isolating the inhabitants from the hustle and bustle of the surrounding streets. ⑦ **St Mary-the-Boltons** (also by Godwin), is perfectly set in the central gardens. It has an unusual spire circled with angels and was extensively restored after bomb damage. ⑧ **Tregunter Road**, part of the Gunter Estate, and several of the nearby streets – Gilston, Priory, Gledhow – take their names from places in Wales and Yorkshire where the family had property. ⑨ **The Society of Authors** (No. 84), founded in 1884 by William Besant to promote and defend the interests of authors. Active members in the past have included Shaw, Galsworthy and E.M. Forster. ⑩ **Blakes** (No. 33). Hidden in a Victorian terrace, this exclusive, idiosyncratic hotel is much admired by media folk – stylish and glitzy, it serves good food *à la mode* in the black, mirrored dining-room (**£££**).

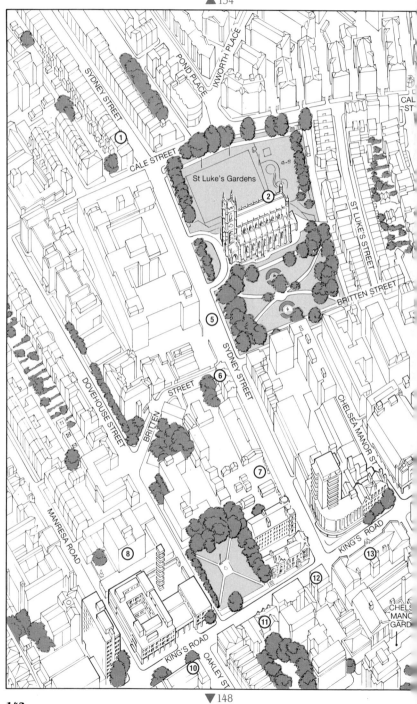

CALE STREET

SYDNEY STREET

POND PLACE

XWORTH PLACE

CAL
ST

ST LUKE'S STREET

St Luke's Gardens

BRITTEN STREET

DOVEHOUSE STREET

BRITTEN STREET

SYDNEY STREET

CHELSEA MANOR ST

MANRESA ROAD

KING'S ROAD

KING'S ROAD

CHELS
MANO
GARD

OAKLEY ST

Sydney Street/King's Road

▲ 135

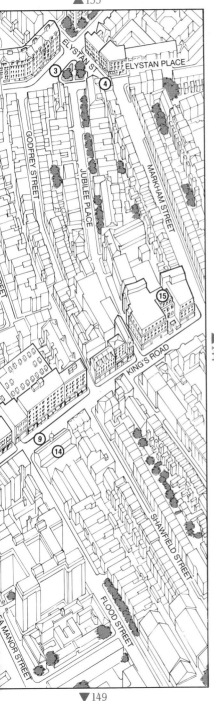

① **The Chelsea Design Co** (65 Sydney St) makes classic English day and evening wear. ② **St Luke's Church** 1820-4, imposing parish church where Dickens was married – an early example of Gothic Revival, by James Savage. ③ The narrow streets of this area, with their glamorized Victorian cottages, have the air of a film-set village, at whose heart, **Chelsea Green**, is ④ **Monkeys** (No. 1), a restaurant popular with well-heeled locals; Anglo-French cuisine (**£££**). ⑤ **Sydney Street** was built in 1845 on Smith's Charity Estate. In 1864 the 'Flying Man', armed with bat wings and a tail, had an undignified crash landing here. ⑥ **Dan's** (No. 119); *nouvelle cuisine* for Sloanes (**££**). ⑦ **The Chelsea Gardener** (No. 125), large expensive garden centre and associated shops. ⑧ **Chelsea School of Art** (sculpture by Henry Moore in the forecourt) nurtures the artistic aspirations of the locals. ⑨ Street-cred clothes shops mingle with fine antique markets along this stretch of the **King's Road**, whilst towards World's End ever more eccentric fashions are brought and paraded. ⑩ **Argyll House**; the first of a row of grand houses, this by Giacomo Leoni, 1723. Recently inhabited by film director Carol Reed. ⑪ **Henry J. Bean's** (No. 195); bar, burgers, floodlit fountain, 1950s American memorabilia (**££**). ⑫ **The Chenil Galleries** (Nos 181-183), specialises in fine arts and rare antiques; note Paul Jones: wonderfully rich antique fabrics. ⑬ **Chelsea Old Town Hall** (1886), listed building by John Brydon with later façade by Leonard Stokes. Inside, murals depict Chelsea's association with the arts, science and literature. It hosts the well-known Antiques Fairs in March and September. ⑭ **Antiquarius** (Nos 135-141), a maze of stalls crammed with every kind of smaller antique – especially good for clothes. Fronting the market are elegant fashion shops, such as **Edina Ronay** (No. 141), for exclusive women's clothes, and **David Fielden** (No. 137) for ravishing evening and wedding dresses. ⑮ **The Pheasantry**: the ornate façade, by the furniture makers Joubert, is all that remains of the original building. It was famous as Princess Astafieva's ballet school, while politicians and painters met in the basement club. Now home to three touristy restaurants, including a basement *tapas* bar (**£**).

▲ 144

▼ 149

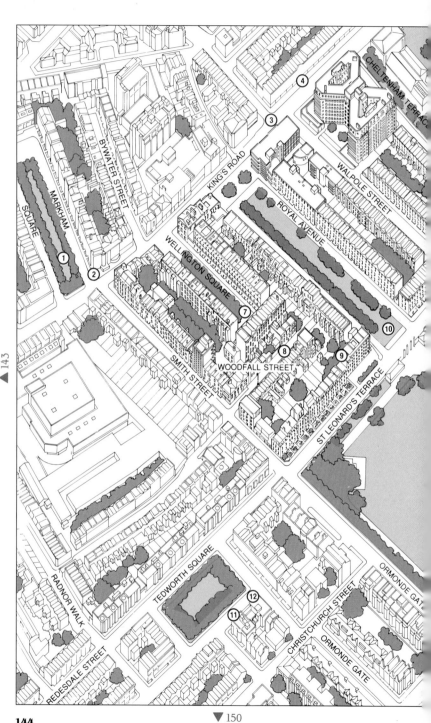

King's Road/Royal Avenue

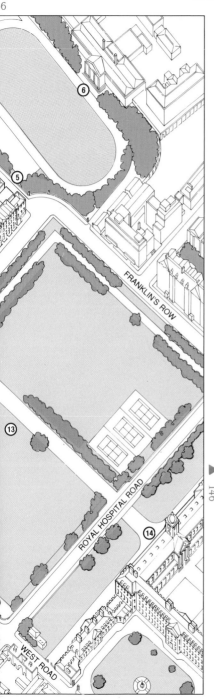

① **Markham Square** (1836) was built on a field belonging to Box Farm, and named after the farm's last owner. ② **Alexander's** basement restaurant (138a King's Road; **££**), a throw-back to the Swinging Sixties when it was owned by the husband of Mary Quant. She occupied the shop above, from where she spearheaded the fashion revolution of 20 years ago. ③ This section of the **King's Road** is dominated by branches of high street fashion chains ④. At No. 98, is the **Chelsea Kitchen** (**£**), cheap, cheerful, honest and, after two decades, something of an institution. ⑤ **Cheltenham Terrace**, a neat row of 18thC houses facing the **Duke of York's** ⑥, administrative headquarters of the Territorial Army and home to various regimental units. The oldest of its buildings, with a central portico, is by John Sanders, 1801, and was built for soldiers' orphans. ⑦ **Wellington Square**, 1830, the earliest of the many squares which opened off the newly public King's Road thoroughfare, and one of the best – well-detailed houses, fine trees. Named after the Duke, whose brother was rector of Chelsea at the time. ⑧ **Woodfall Street**, a green and flowery cul-de-sac of charming 19thC cottages. On the corner, the Phoenix is a quiet, wood-panelled Edwardian pub. ⑨ Bram Stoker, author of *Dracula*, lived at **18 St Leonard's Terrace** at the turn of the century. This block (Nos 14-31) is considered to be one of the best Georgian terraces in Chelsea (1765). ⑩ **Royal Avenue**, a wide boulevard built in 1692-4 (houses are 19thC), part of William III's unfinished plan to link the Royal Hospital with his new residence, Kensington Palace. Fictional home of James Bond. ⑪ **23 Tedworth Square**, home of Mark Twain briefly 1896-7; now flats. ⑫ **No. 15**, home of two actresses, first Lillie Langtry and later Mrs Patrick Campbell, who received G.B. Shaw's famous correspondence at this address. ⑬ **Burton's Court**, 14 acres of open land, not open to the public; Chelsea Pensioners play bowls and the Brigade of Guards play cricket here. ⑭ 'Quiet, dignified, the work of a gentleman'. Carlyle's description of the **Royal Hospital** founded by Charles II for veteran soldiers (the Chelsea Pensioners with their distinctive uniforms) and built by Wren 1682-92. Chapel, Hall and grounds (*see page 147*) open to the public.

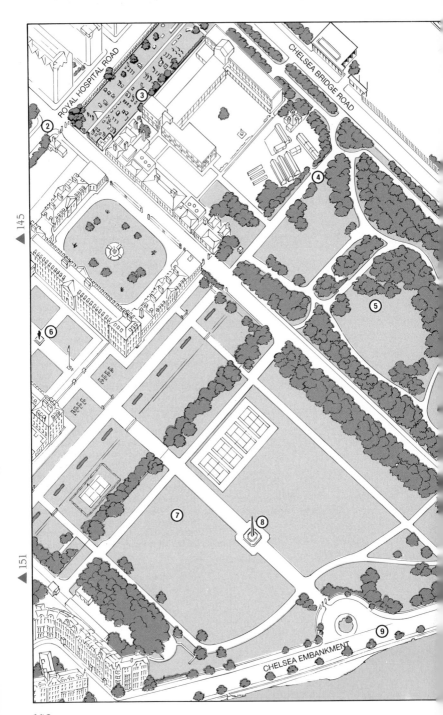

ROYAL HOSPITAL ROAD

CHELSEA BRIDGE ROAD

CHELSEA EMBANKMENT

146

Ranelagh Gardens

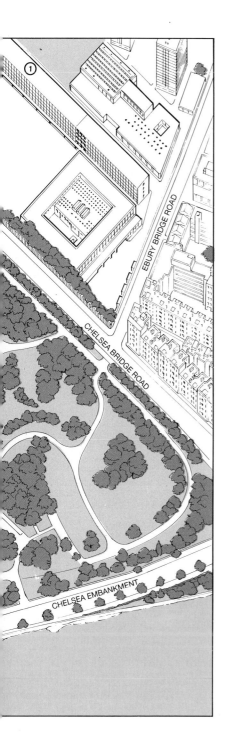

① **Chelsea Barracks**, first built by George Moore in 1861-2 for 1000 footguards, then rebuilt in the 1960s by Tripe and Wakeham. ② **Royal Hospital Road**, originally called Queen's Road and lined with many fine houses, now demolished. ③ The last resting place for Chelsea Pensioners, **Royal Hospital Burial Ground** was consecrated in 1691 and closed for burials in 1854. Among the 10,000 buried here are William Hiseland, a Pensioner who died in 1732 at the ripe old age of 112, and two women who joined the army, and whose sex was only discovered when they were wounded in the Crimean War. ④ **Site of Ranelagh House**, a mansion built c1690 by the Earl of Ranelagh, Paymaster-General to the Forces. After the earl's death, the house and grounds, ⑤ **Ranelagh Gardens**, were bought by a syndicate, and in 1742 the grounds were opened to the public as pleasure gardens. Until they closed in 1803, the gardens were reputedly the most fashionable and elegant in Europe. Gothic novelist, Horace Walpole, claimed: 'You can't set your foot without treading on a Prince, or Duke of Cumberland.' Attractions included music, opera, Venetian masquerades, boating on an artificial lake, stalls selling Dresden, booths serving refreshments, a magnificent rococo rotunda and a Chinese pavilion. ⑥ Grinling Gibbons's bronze **statue of Charles II** dressed as a Roman soldier gave Figure Court its name. On Oak-apple Day, 29 May, the Chelsea Pensioners decorate the statue with oak leaves to celebrate the King's birthday, and his escape from the Roundheads at Worcester, hidden in an oak tree. ⑦ The **grounds of the Royal Hospital** (*see page 145*), designed by Wren as a formal garden have, since 1913, been the scene of the Chelsea Flower Show each May. ⑧ Charles Cockerell's towering **granite obelisk** (1853) commemorates the soldiers who fell at Chillianwalla in January 1849. ⑨ **Chelsea Embankment**. Along with Albert and Victoria embankments, an impressive Victorian achievement (with main sewers below); work of Sir Joseph Bazalgette.

147

▲142

CARLYLE SQUARE

KING'S ROAD

BRAMERTON STREET

GLEBE PLACE

MARGARETTA TERRACE

FLOOD WALK

PHENE STREET

OAKLEY STREET

UPPER CHEYNE ROW

CHEYNE ROW

JUSTICE WALK

OLD CHURCH STREET

LAWRENCE STREET

CHEYNE WALK

CHELSEA EMBANKMENT

Roper's Garden

RIVER THAMES
CHELSEA REACH

Cheyne Walk/Oakley Street

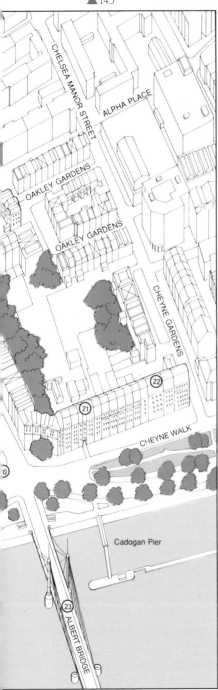

① Osbert Sitwell lived at **No. 2** in leafy, elegant Carlyle Square. ② **Chelsea Antique Market** (Nos 245-253), good for bargains, bric-à-brac and books. ③ **No. 215**, attractive brick house (1720), occupied by Dr T. Arne, composer of *Rule Britannia*, and later by actress Ellen Terry. ④ Charles Kingsley, author of *The Water Babies*, lived at **St Luke's Rectory** (56 Old Church Street) as a child. ⑤ **Phené Arms**, one of Chelsea's oldest pubs, built by local eccentric, Dr Phené ⑥ Pretty, flat-fronted **22 Upper Cheyne Row** was home of critic Leigh Hunt. ⑦ Roman Catholic **Church of St Thomas More** (1895), built on the site of a William de Morgan pottery. ⑧ In the mid-18thC, picaresque novelist Smollett lived at **16 Lawrence Street**, which also housed the Chelsea China factory. ⑨ **Grey House Books** (No. 12a), charming antiquarian bookshop. ⑩ ' ... flag-pathed, sunk-storied, iron-railed, all old-fashioned': Scottish historian and philosopher Thomas Carlyle's description of Cheyne Row, where he lived at ⑪ **No. 24**, a handsome Queen Anne house crammed with his possessions (open in summer). ⑫ **Oakley Street**, built on the Cadogan Estate in the 1850s. Oscar Wilde sought refuge with his mother and brother at No. 87 during his persecution; Antarctic explorer, Robert Falcon Scott, lived at No. 56. ⑬ **Old Church Street**, Chelsea's oldest thoroughfare. ⑭ **H. Allen Smith** (No. 26), wine merchants since 1832, originally occupied the old court-house in Justice Walk ⑮, where the cells were used as cellars. ⑯ **Crosby Hall** (fine hammerbeam roof, plus Holbein's *Sir Thomas More and Family*) is the great hall of a 15thC mansion, moved here piecemeal from Bishopsgate in 1910 to escape demolition (open daily). ⑰ **Roper's Gardens**, named after More's daughter, Margaret Roper. ⑱ Before their state wedding, Henry VIII married Jane Seymour in **Chelsea Old Church** (1157, but much rebuilt). ⑲ 400-year-old pub, **King's Head and Eight Bells**. Outside what is now a car showroom is Wynne's graceful sculpture ⑳ **Boy with a Dolphin**. ㉑ **Nos 19-26**, site of Henry VIII's manor house. Mulberry trees said to be planted by Elizabeth I can be glimpsed through the arch of No. 24. ㉒ **No. 16**, home of Rossetti and Swinburne, who lived with a menagerie of exotic animals, including peacocks whose screeches disturbed the neighbours. ㉓ **Albert Bridge**, Ordish's pretty cantilever and suspension bridge, with tollhouses still intact (1873).

▲ 144

▲ 149

RIVER THAMES
CHELSEA REACH

Royal Hospital Road/Chelsea Embankment

▲145

▼146

① **The Surprise**, popular 'local' with prints of old Chelsea on the walls. ② **National Army Museum**, purpose-built and opened in 1971. History of the British Army from Henry VII to the present day; models, dioramas, weapons, uniforms, paintings. ③ **La Tante Claire** (No. 68), Pierre Koffmann's summery, understated temple of modern French gastronomy (**£££**). ④ **Swan Walk**, cluster of graceful 18thC houses, set back. Walton's *Façade* was first performed in one, briefly inhabited by Edith Sitwell 1917-19. ⑤ In **Tite Street**, the scene of much artistic endeavour, No. 35, The White House (now replaced) was built by avant-garde architect Edward Godwin for Whistler (*see page 153*) in 1877, but he had to leave due to his libel case with Ruskin. ⑥ **No. 33**, Augustus John's studios. ⑦ **No. 31**, home of American artist John Singer Sargent, who died here. ⑧ **No. 34**, Oscar Wilde's marital home from 1884 to his arrest in 1895. It was suitably aesthetically decorated by Godwin (who also designed No. 44, The Tower House). ⑨ **Cheyne Walk**, elegant, much coveted single row of tall, mainly Queen Anne houses, built on the site of Henry VIII's Chelsea Manor, which was subsequently owned by the Cheyne and then the Sloane family. Until it became separated from the embankment, this was a bustling riverside street, which attracted a remarkable catalogue of famous residents (notable in modern times: Mick Jagger, Lord Weidenfeld, Paul Getty II, Gerald Scarfe) from artists, musicians and writers to eccentrics and misers (*see also pages 149 and 153*). ⑩ **No. 4** (fine ironwork and doorway) is where the elderly, newly married George Eliot died. ⑪ **Nos 7-11** date from the 1880s; David Lloyd George lived in No. 10. ⑫ **Chelsea Physic Garden** (open two afternoons in summer and during Chelsea Flower Show), botanical gardens established in 1673 by the Society of Apothecaries; exotic trees, shrubs and herbs. ⑬ Fine houses along this stretch of Chelsea Embankment (*see page 147*) include **Nos 18, 17, 15, 11, 10, 9 and 8** (notice the clock) by Richard Norman Shaw, leading exponent of the 'Queen Anne style' in London (c1870s), and **Nos 6, 5 and 4** by Godwin (conventional for him). ⑭ **London Peace Pagoda**, 1985, built in Battersea Park by Japanese Buddhist monks, a tranquil addition to the riverside.

WORLD'S END PASSAGE

CHEYNE WALK

CHEYNE WALK

RIVER THAMES

BATTERSEA REACH

LOTS ROAD

Cheyne Walk/Lots Road

① **World's End Passage** once approached a 17thC inn bearing the same name, and a tea garden. It is now engulfed by a large housing estate which incorporates ② the **Chelsea Towers** complex. World's End is the western boundary of Chelsea. ③ At **119 Cheyne Walk** (*see also pages 149 and 151*) the eccentric and elderly J.M.W. Turner, found solitude and anonymity under the name of Booth. He died there in 1851. ④ **Isardi**, No. 112, a smart Italian restaurant (**££**), curves around Munroe Terrace. ⑤ **Nos 109** and **108** were the homes, earlier this century, of the painter Philip Wilson Steer and the sculptor John Tweed respectively. ⑥ Hilaire Belloc lived at **No. 104** between 1901 and 1905. ⑦ **No. 101** was the first of ten Chelsea addresses for the American painter Whistler. He called Chelsea 'the wonderful village', and stayed from 1862 until his death in 1903. ⑧ A cream-coloured country mansion, **Lindsey House**, Nos 96-100, is the only reminder of the days when Chelsea was known as a 'Town of Palaces' (Defoe). Built c1674 as the seat of the Earl of Lindsey, it was subdivided into five houses in the 1770s, and has embraced as residents Count Zinzendorf and his Moravian community (a failure), the engineers Brunel, father (Marc Isambard) and son (Isambard Kingdom) and Whistler (again). ⑨ **Nos 91-95** are notable: Nos 91 and 92 have attractive Venetian windows, and No. 91 a glazed first-floor veranda. Mrs Gaskell was born at No. 93 in 1810. ⑩ Bazalgette's 1880s wrought-iron **Battersea Bridge** replaced an earlier wooden one often depicted by Whistler. It links Battersea with Chelsea, at the point where Sir Thomas More's 16thC country estate once stood. ⑪ Gaily painted houseboats line the **Chelsea Basin**. ⑫ **Cremorne Gardens**, a welcome open space overlooking the river, commemorates the pleasure gardens which started life in 1832 as a sporting stadium (hence Stadium Street) and evolved into a delightful open-air centre of 19thC entertainments: balloon ascents, fireworks, pageants, grottoes and music. They closed in 1877 and today only an ornate iron entrance gate remains, now displayed in the present garden. ⑬ **Chelsea Wharf**, a flour mill converted to offices, studios, a sprinkling of shops and a Chinese restaurant, Dynasty, (**££**). Also the London Wine Co: wines by the case. ⑭ **Chelsea Harbour**, a yuppified, sanitized fantasy 'riverside village' development, built around a yacht basin beyond Chelsea Creek (off map). The '80s boom over, it is eerily quiet, but there are a couple of good restaurants, **Deals** and Marco Pierre White's **Canteen** (**££**).

Greenwich

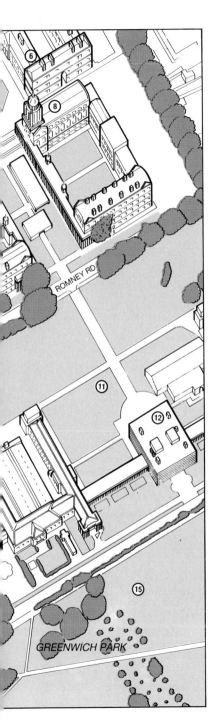

ROMNEY RD

GREENWICH PARK

① Victorian-tiled **Greenwich Footway Tunnel**, linking Greenwich to the Isle of Dogs. ② Site of **Greenwich Palace**. Built in 1427 by Henry V's brother, the Duke of Gloucester, it was the scene of Tudor banquets, jousting tournaments and hunting parties. Wren demolished it to build the Royal Naval Hospital (now the Royal Naval College). ③ Marble **statue of George II** in Roman dress by J. M. Rysbrack (1735). ④ **King Charles's Quarters**, oldest part of the Royal Naval College, built in 1664 by John Webb (a pupil of Inigo Jones) as a wing of a new palace, which remained unfinished due to lack of funds. ⑤ Almost 30 years later, Queen Mary commissioned Wren to build a naval hospital. The hospital closed in 1869, and in 1873 the **Royal Naval College** moved here from Portsmouth. ⑥ **Queen Anne's Quarters** (1728), built by Vanbrugh, who succeeded Wren and used his plans, beneath which is the undercroft of Greenwich Palace. **Gipsy Moth IV** (off map), a 53ft ketch in which Sir Francis Chichester sailed solo around the world in 1966-7. ⑦ **Cutty Sark**, magnificent 19thC tea clipper, the fastest of its kind, has a display of historical documents and a wonderful collection of figureheads. ⑧ In Queen Mary's Quarter, Wren's **Chapel** was damaged by fire and restored with a delicate rococo interior by James 'Athenian' Stuart. ⑨ **Painted Hall** (1727) in King William's Quarter, where Sir James Thornhill's vast baroque paintings, celebrating Britain's Protestant monarchy, decorate the ceiling of Wren's domed building. ⑩ **Dreadnought Seamen's Hospital**, built by 'Athenian' Stuart in 1763. ⑪ **National Maritime Museum**, where exhibits range from decorated royal river boats to Turner paintings, is centred on ⑫ **Queen's House**, Inigo Jones's perfect Palladian villa recently renovated. ⑬ **King's Arms**, pub with nautical prints and a pleasant garden. ⑭ Hawksmoor church, **St Alfege's** (1718), marks the site of the martyrdom of the Archbishop of Canterbury at the hands of the Danes in 1012. ⑮ **Greenwich Park**, the beautiful grounds of Greenwich Palace, added to the estate in 1433 and landscaped by Le Nôtre in Charles II's reign. ⑯ **Greenwich Theatre**, a 19thC music-hall, rebuilt in 1969. Other buildings of interest are the Old Royal Observatory and Flamsteed House, both by Wren, the Meridian Building and Ranger's House, both 18thC (all off map).

GENERAL POINTS OF INTEREST

PEOPLE OF INTEREST

A

STREET NAMES

Y

Z